Praise for *The*

'Acutely evocative . . . Ripples with
feel as though their author has r
out something you have been o
i Newspaper

'What Cosslett so beautifully captures is that liminal period
before any life-changing decision, when anguished uncertainty
morphs into sudden resolve'
New Statesman

'Sharp and accurate . . . a brave process of healing
and self-reconstruction'
Observer

'A powerful argument for the way a pet can create a feeling of
stability in an unequal and often atomised society and work
culture. Her observations are sharp and accurate . . . The book is
not then so much a cosy ode to cats and cat ladies as an honest
examination of Cosslett's traumatised yet resilient self'
Guardian

'This clear-eyed and thoughtful book examines everything from
the aftermath of a shock assault to the chaos of lockdown while
asking questions about what makes us invest in the things
and places we love and why they are so necessary for us
to thrive . . . tender and uplifting'
Stylist

'A meditative read on what it means not just to be a mother, but
a human being just trying to navigate all that life throws at us'
Red Online

'I loved it. Such a strong, nuanced book; Rhiannon's writing
is as sharp as her thinking. It's funny, human, rich
with thought and care'
Rebecca Watson, author of *Little Scratch*

'The most beautiful paragraphs in *The Year of the Cat* remind me what a rare gift Rhiannon Lucy Cosslett possesses: expansive compassion, empathy and warmth, but a scalpel precision with words. Memories are conjured so headily it feels, to the reader, less like reading than experiencing déjà vu'
Emma Forrest, author of *Busy Being Free*

'A nuanced calibration of care, desire, trauma and anxiety that made me feel so energised. A superbly written, special book'
Olivia Sudjic, author of *Asylum Road*

'Such a moving, unique and elegant book, examining mental health, motherhood, creativity, love, life, youth, femininity, family and friendship. But above all, Cosslett takes her place in a long history of genius writers in the meowmoir genre by celebrating her strong bond with a true hero – Mackerel the cat. I loved this book, and if you have a heart, you will, too'
Nick Bradley, author of *The Cat and the City*

'A tender and wise meditation on trauma and the fragmentation of memory. Weaving together a history of women and their feline companions, Cosslett charts the emergence of a lasting love, while grappling with deeper anxieties: what it means to be a carer, and a mother, in precarious times. With her signature wit and radiant prose, Cosslett has produced a remarkable work, one that speaks for her generation'
Jessica Cornwell, author of *Birth Notes*

'I feel like I have been waiting my whole life for this brilliant book, alive with Rhiannon's characteristic blend of gorgeous prose, razor-sharp analysis and enormous amounts of empathy and honesty. You'll come back to it again and again, as I have'
Lucia Osborne-Crowley, author of *I Choose Elena*

Rhiannon Lucy Cosslett writes columns and reviews fiction for the *Guardian*, and has also written for the *Observer Magazine*, *i newspaper*, *Vogue*, *TIME*, the *New Statesman*, *Stylist*, *Elle* and many other publications. She is the author of a novel, *The Tyranny of Lost Things*. Raised in Wales, she now lives in north London.

THE YEAR
OF THE CAT

Rhiannon Lucy Cosslett

TINDER
PRESS

First published in Great Britain in 2023 by Tinder Press
An imprint of HEADLINE PUBLISHING GROUP

First published in paperback in 2023 by Tinder Press
An imprint of HEADLINE PUBLISHING GROUP

1

Cataloguing in Publication Data is available from the British Library

Mass Market Paperback ISBN 978 1 4722 9074 8

Typeset in Scala by Palimpsest Book Production Ltd, Falkirk, Stirlingshire

Printed and bound in Great Britain by Clays Ltd, Elcograf S.p.A.

HEADLINE PUBLISHING GROUP
An Hachette UK Company
Carmelite House
50 Victoria Embankment
London EC4Y 0DZ

www.tinderpress.co.uk
www.headline.co.uk
www.hachette.co.uk

For all the cat women

'Whether I want kids is a secret I keep from myself – it
is the greatest secret that I keep from myself'
– Sheila Heti, *Motherhood*

'If at any point in my life I was able to find out what the
future held, I would always have wanted to know whether
or not I would have children. More than love, more than
work, more than length of life or quantity
of happiness, this was the question whose mystery
I found the most compelling'
– Rachel Cusk, *A Life's Work*

'Time spent with a cat is never wasted'
– Colette

A cat lady is a cultural archetype or stock character, most often depicted as a woman, a middle-aged or elderly spinster, who has many cats. The term may be pejorative, or it may be affectionately embraced.

I

Spring

The kitten's eyes are just on the cusp of changing from blue to green. In the tiny, blurred square of a video that I am for some reason unable to maximise, and which has been filmed in the wrong aspect ratio, she stands apart from her baby siblings, all of whom are wrestling while emitting high-pitched mews that are almost mouse-like in sound. In contrast, she is still, with a worried-looking expression on her face – eyes wide, mouth and whiskers downturned – a kitten in need of some love. She looks like a mix of every cat going – a tortoiseshell with flashes of white on her forehead, bib and feet, offset with the most beautiful patches of café au lait. My husband has already said he likes her the best.

I send the video to my friend Jacob. 'It's her,' I say. 'It's her that we want.'

'The existential-looking one in the corner?' he types.

Yes. She's the one.

What is it about a cat's face that makes it so lovable? Experts have suggested that their features are appealingly human-looking, reminding us of babies' countenances. The cat-worshipping internet calls cats and other pets 'fur babies', a phrase that I would rather die than ever use, but nonetheless, perhaps this hints at some truth. A young Emily Brontë wrote an essay in which she argued that 'the cat, although it differs in some physical points, is extremely like us in disposition'. This is because, like humans, a cat is able to hide its true feelings: 'in its own interest,' she writes, '[a cat] sometimes hides its misanthropy under the guise of amiable gentleness'.

Though human-like – heart-shaped, with a small nose and large, forward-facing eyes – a cat's face is not expressive, and perhaps this is what makes the cat a better liar. This deadpan expression is also what makes the cat so hilarious. It's a face that demands to be taken seriously, juxtaposed with a body that can move clumsily through the world, tearing down curtains and colliding with plate-glass windows with slapstick inelegance. It's within this disconnect, I believe, that you find the true essence of cat.

Sometimes, usually when I'm among strangers who live outside of the city, I am asked why I do not have children. It is a seemingly innocent question, but as far as I know, it is not one that is often asked of my husband.

However kindly it is meant, I hear within it the seed of another question: *'What is your purpose?'*

We only ever hear of cat ladies; never of cat men. Historically, the temperaments of women were frequently compared

4

with those of felines, and sexist quotations on the subject are easy to find, for example: 'A woman is a perfidious tricky cat, with claws and fangs, an enemy in love who will bite him when she is tired of kisses' (Guy de Maupassant, 'On Cats', 1886). Or: 'An animal that makes the night her day, and who shocks decent people with the noise of her orgies, can only have one single analogy in the world, and that analogy is of the feminine kind' (Alphonse Toussenel, *Passional Zoology*, 1852).

There are old, old links between cats and women. In ancient Egypt, the feline goddess Bastet represented fertility and childbirth, and was often depicted with a litter of kittens. As well as being nurturing, there was also the potential for violence and destruction (anyone who has seen a cat's mood change from affectionate to aggressive on the turn of a hair will understand this). Just like the sun, with its power over feast or famine, Bastet had the potential to both give life and take it away. She started out as a lion-headed goddess, before morphing into a more domestic cat or cat-headed woman around the 2nd millennium BCE.

The Greek goddess Hecate, goddess of the moon and magic, necromancy and sorcery, had a familiar called Galinthias. Galinthias was a deceitful woman who, having lied to the gods in an attempt to save her friend from the continuous birth pains wrought upon her by the Fates and the goddess of childbirth, was punished by being turned into a cat. Another myth sees the goddess Artemis transformed into a cat while fleeing Egypt, taking refuge in the moon.

The Phrygian mother-goddess Cybele had a chariot drawn by lions, and in Norse mythology, the fertility goddess Freja is hauled around in a cat-drawn chariot (her goddess powers must have been extensive, because it is difficult to imagine a less cooperative herd of servants, hence the expression 'like herding cats').

These old links between cats and motherhood make sense when you consider the fecundity of the female cat – she can produce as many as five litters a year, which sounds like a harrowing ordeal. I remember this fact whenever I turn away from the grimness of the news to look enviously upon my cat, sleeping peacefully, oblivious.

(I have been around exhausted new mothers – have seen how their fraying nerves dwell close to the surface. 'I just want to be able to take a dump on my own,' one, a friend of a friend, said when we bumped into her in the park. 'And *they've* been no help at all.' She didn't seem to care that the 'they' in question – her 'fucking useless' husband and parents-in-law – were standing just behind her. Her filter had gone.)

The kitten looks a little bit like the first cat that was ever truly mine. As a baby, I lived with two cats, Smith and The Minx, in a co-op house that had once been a squat (my

6

parents were there too, but they are not central to this story). I can't remember either of these cats, but I do suspect that living with them from birth onwards led to my abiding feeling that a home is not truly a home without a cat.

Furthermore, I was born in what is, essentially, a cat-themed hospital. The Whittington, in north London, is named after the fourteenth century adventurer who came to London, cat in tow. The walls of the hospital are decorated with colourful cats, there is a statue of the cat outside, and the nearby park has cat-shaped topiary.

When I was five, some friends from the countryside brought me a tortoiseshell farm kitten. By that stage, Smith, understandably traumatised by being moved to another city, had become semi-feral and disappeared.

I named the farm kitten Molly, and I would lose her in a similar fashion just two years later.

The story of a pet is, to an extent, always a story about mortality. We buy children pets in order to help them come to terms with this concept, and for many of us, the death of a beloved animal is our first significant loss.

'Grief for a pet is grief for the vanishing of the tiny unknowable universe that is her consciousness; but it's also grief for a part of your own life,' wrote the critic Sam Leith, in a moving elegy to his cat Henry (we writers are at home a lot, and so spend many hours with our cats).

I live a stone's throw from where I was born. My neighbourhood is a cat's paradise. They are everywhere: curled up on doorsteps, frolicking in flowerbeds, gazing sternly out from windows. However, it is also a death trap, a ruthlessly demarcated badlands that cats must learn to cross while retaining all their limbs. It is *Saving Private Ryan*, for cats.

In summer, when the windows are thrown wide open, you will often be yanked from your balmy reverie by a sudden cacophony of yowls. What you're hearing is either a catfight or a cat-versus-fox stand-off. These altercations rarely end well, if the 'Lost Cat' posters that paper our neighbourhood are anything to go by. 'Please check your sheds,' these posters always say, but we never discover whether or not the cats turn up. I like to think they do, but I suspect that most do not.

I have lived in this flat for almost a decade, and for most of that time, we were sandwiched between two cats, one in the downstairs flat and one in the upstairs. Both were, in their own ways, bruisers. Seriously, you did not fuck with these cats, and you certainly wouldn't have wanted to introduce a kitten to the building. I told myself that this was the reason I never got round to getting my own, but the truth was that my life never felt stable enough.

My experience of pets and mortality had been extensive: as a child, I had hamsters, which everyone knows are essentially designed to die. My first hamster, called Geri, because she was ginger, was mistakenly buried alive by my father while she was hibernating. I only discovered this fact as an adult. My mother said that my father, an animal-loving vegetarian, wore a haunted expression for days after he realised.

(Ask people about their hamster deaths. They are rarely run-of-the-mill. A friend – a woman who once lectured me on a Sicilian pavement for eating a barbecued horse burger – once confessed that, as a young child, she'd killed her hamster by playing table tennis with it. I had asked her, 'What's the worst thing you've ever done?' It took me a minute to process her answer. First, I imagined the hamster as a worthy opponent across the net. Then . . . *Oh*. She was near tears when she told me this shameful secret, and blamed her 'psychopathic' brother.)

My second hamster, Fluffy, went bald, ironically enough, then also died. That Fluffy had lived so long was already a miracle, because he had escaped from his cage and been at large in our home for several weeks, somehow evading our two cats. No one seemed to think it was particularly unusual that we spent a significant period of time living alongside a small rodent. My mother left food out for him in the evenings. He must have grown tired of this outlaw existence, though, because one morning I looked in his cage and there he was.

But the biggest loss was Molly. She had been removed from her territory and, as is often the case with cats, we suspect she died trying to return to it. Cats, like humans, need a stable home.

Home has always been important to me. When I left at eighteen, to go to Paris, I cried for ten days. I had not expected it, and the woman whose children I was looking after was bemused at the blotchy, tear-soaked British girl who turned up and asked to use the landline to phone her mother more than was necessary (by which I mean a couple of times a week that first month – my new employer was not a sentimentalist). The emotional outpouring also surprised my mother, because I had skipped off with hardly a second thought, having arranged the whole thing myself.

I believe now that I was reeling.

In her masterpiece *On Cats*, Doris Lessing writes of the long period she spent catless, saying: 'Cats had no place in an existence spent always moving from place to place, room to room. A cat needs a place as much as it needs a person to make its own.'

Throughout my twenties, my life felt temporary, and I was not alone: one friend counted that she had moved twenty-five times in less than a decade. The newspapers call us 'generation rent'. Certainly, we feel rootless, dogged by the possibility of eviction with just a few weeks' notice; afraid of the damage a pet could do to our precious security deposits. In my twenties, my only friend with a cat was Holly, and she's one of those people who accumulates cats wherever she goes without much of a say in the arrangement. Really, the cat chose her.

It may seem strange to be writing of instability when I have lived in the same place for ten years now, but that wasn't how I ever expected it to turn out. For most of this time, the lease was on a rolling one-month contract (also, my name was not on it), and the flat was shared with a parade of friends and strangers who, my mother said, seemed to make up half the guests at our eventual wedding. The flatmate who became my husband spent years on a temporary work contract, and I made my living from a combination of freelance and casual work. It felt as though the rug could be pulled from under us at any minute. To bring a cat, let alone anything as demanding as a baby, into that environment felt irresponsible, and wrong.

And yet, every now and again, I would scroll the online classifieds for kittens.

I was also going mad. It's important to mention this. There are better ways of putting it: I was suffering extreme psychological distress, I was mentally ill, I had post-traumatic stress disorder – you can take your pick. But none of them seem to properly convey the truth of the matter: I was completely insane.

Though there were long periods where I was functioning, madness bookended my twenties. When I was twenty-three, a man tried to kill me, and the trauma of that caused a rupture in my brain. Then, at twenty-seven, my proximity to the Paris terror attacks prodded the trauma awake and the madness returned, worse than ever before.

I lived in a state of hypervigilance. It felt, I wrote at the time, as though I was an animal, flinching at every small noise. And I recognise it in others, or I did in normal times, when I was out and about in the city. I would see someone jump out of their skin, on the street or on the bus, because of some unexpected sound or gesture, and I would know: *Something happened to you.* The body remembers and reacts long before the brain, jolting and twitching in terror just as it did during its initial onslaught. Even years later, in the safety of my own home, I will startle to see my husband appearing unexpectedly in a doorway, or will cry out involuntarily if surprised.

When, in the middle of a pandemic-induced lockdown, we brought the kitten home, I came to understand this fully. The way she startled at the slightest movement, her ears pricking up, her body readying itself for fight or flight as she wound it in like a spring ready to launch, when all I'd done was something as innocuous as turning on a light: I had felt that. A misfiring.

Though I had all these very valid reasons not to get a cat, I still wanted one. Thankfully, the internet existed, and everyone knows that cats are the lifeblood of the internet.

I took solace in cat videos, in Bodega Cats and Medieval Cats, in subreddits such as r/SupermodelCats ('very good-looking photogenic cats' – it wouldn't be the internet if its citizens, however furry they may be, were not held to ruthless physical standards), and in cat influencers, many of whom are 'chonky' (internet speak for obese). Grumpy cat (RIP) was always a bit too mainstream for me, though of course I was a fan of the original 'I CAN HAZ CHEEZBURGER' lolcat. I also appreciated memes including left-field forum pictures of cats photobombing other cats. A favourite, which was my desktop background for a good five years, showed a cat open-mouthed in the foreground, as if horrified and traumatised, while, in the background, another cat mounts a third. I still laugh every time I look at it.

For a long time, these cats were enough.

When we were in our early twenties, my friends and I used to joke about becoming crazy cat ladies. 'I just want to live alone with my cats,' we would moan, having slept with the third, or the fourth, or the eleventh man who never called, or who turned out to have a girlfriend, or a secret baby, or a weird fetish, or to be one of those guys – of which there are many – who do not own a single towel ('How do you dry yourself?' we'd ask, aghast, to which they'd reply: 'I drip dry'). We were exhausted from the labour of trying to find someone normal, and to become a crazy cat lady was not so much an admission of defeat as it was a retreat from a game that felt rigged against us.

We knew that 'crazy' was one of the worst things that a woman could be; were too young to understand that, when a man proclaims his ex-girlfriend a 'psycho', it can often say more about him than it does about her. (Now, we might think: *Hmm, yes, but did you make her that way? Did you subject her to years of gaslighting? Or did she ultimately crack and scream at you in the deli queue not because she is mentally unstable, but because you slept with her for a year and a half, only to inform her that you have a girlfriend when she finally asks if you can meet her parents?*)

We gave the vision of the crazy cat lady a certain glamorous sheen: our cat-owning spinsters were not lonely older women abandoned by a failing mental health system, but Holly Golightlys, with their cats curled around their necks like living stoles, offset by diamonds. We had the *Breakfast at Tiffany's* poster on our walls, showing Audrey Hepburn in a black cocktail dress as she poses with her cat perched on her shoulder, a 'slob without a name' who, like her glamorous girl-about-town owner, cannot, it seems, be tamed.

In *Breakfast at Tiffany's*, Holly Golightly is like a cat herself: stubbornly independent, semi-nocturnal, and, in her embodiment by Hepburn, feline in appearance. She is young and beautiful, and so were we, though we had too many hang-ups to realise it then; it was only later we looked back on photographs of ourselves and marvelled that we had ever felt fat.

14

The crazy cat lady was just a spectre that we joked about. She loomed at a juncture so far in the future as to be unimaginable. We did not know what it was to age, and as for our fertility, we only thought about it when we were freaking out about accidental pregnancy while washing down the morning-after pill with our hangovers. We were closer to Golightly than to Grey Gardens, and though we flitted from feckless man to feckless man, we didn't truly fear becoming crazy cat ladies, because we were sure that romantic commitment and its attendant offspring would one day be ours. We remembered the happy ending from the film: that trench-coat kiss in the rain while she holds the cat in her arms, not the novella's more ambiguous ending: a postcard from Argentina, another married man and no place to live.

It would all be fine: we had so much time. We could have it all, and fifty dollars for the powder room.

Champfleurette, the White Cat, Louise Bourgeois' high-heeled cat alter ego, embodies the cat as a sexual, minx-like creature of the night. A feminisation of Champfleury, the art critic who produced a cat book in the 1890s that includes drawings from Manet, Champfleurette is named after one of the two cats Bourgeois owned while living on New York's 18th Street (the other was called Tyger). In the image, Champfleurette's exaggerated backside is raised lasciviously in the air. Of the work, Bourgeois said: 'There is a kind of disassociation between what the girl thinks . . . that is, what she wishes . . . and what she appears to be. What she wishes is to be a goody-goody . . . but the document reveals that her deeper mind is on something completely different!'

In her poem 'Ella Mason and Her Eleven Cats', Sylvia Plath writes of a local cat lady who was once fashionable, 'minx-thin' and beautiful, but is now a solitary spinster 'run to fat'.

Mason is a figure of fear for Plath and her childhood friends, and it is recounted how they would spy upon and mock her. Her rejection of men is deemed the reason for her loneliness and possible alcoholism. But with time, Plath and the other children grow 'kinder', recognising that she can be set against those 'girls who marry' who 'need no lesson', perhaps not because she had standards that were too high, but because of her refusal to compromise.

I read that nearly three-quarters of animal hoarders are women. Animal hoarding appears in the *Diagnostic and Statistical Manual of Mental Disorders*, classified as a subtype of a psychiatric disorder. 'There's a crazy cat lady on every street,' a pet detective, Colin Butcher, who specialises in returning stolen cats to their owners, tells a newspaper reporter. 'They are always women.' No one ever seems to blame the cats, who are bigamous by nature, and have been known to have at least four other secret families, all of whom believe the cat to be theirs. My father once looked out of the front window to see our cat gazing impassively back at him from the house opposite, as if to say: *What?*

(A photo from a property listing recently went viral when the neighbour who was looking at it pointed out that the ginger cat sprawled shamelessly on the bed was his own.)

New babies often cause cats to relocate. Perhaps cats favour child-free women just as much as child-free women favour cats.

There's a grainy meme, a photograph showing a crowd of cats assembled on the threshold of someone's front door. *HI, WE UNDERSTAND YOU ARE 40*, it says, *AND STILL NOT MARRIED.*

When one of my colleagues, who does not have children, was called a 'crazy cat lady' by a male journalist, she retorted that it was 'slut-shaming for the over thirties'.

There are attempts to rehabilitate the image of the cat lady. One of my favourite modern photography projects is *Girls and their Cats*, a book of photographs by BriAnne Wills that emphasises the creativity, coolness and diversity of women who own and love cats. Another photographer,

Brooke Hummer, photographed women and their cats in the style of historical paintings ranging from nineteenth-century colonial to surrealist, subverting the shaming stereotype of the cat lady and reinterpreting the way Western art has portrayed women. The pictures in her *Cat Women* series are beautiful, celebratory, and hilarious. My favourite is a pastiche of a medieval painting of the Madonna and child. A tabby with a halo sits in the crook of the subject's arm, where the baby Jesus would be. It appeals to me because it's an amusing twist on the endless slides of early Renaissance religious paintings that we were shown in dusty, soporific lecture halls at university, and also because it makes me feel part of a tribe of cat women who somewhat jokingly treat their pets as surrogate children.

Still, the stereotype prevails.

I was twenty-three when I met my husband, which seems terribly young now. By the time I found him, I had been involved with boys and then men in one way or another for nearly a decade, and had become jaded. I'd tried all kinds of men: men who were older than I, men who were artists, men who were chefs, Italian men, men with pasts, men with alcohol problems, men who quoted philosophy after sex, men who thought Germaine Greer was a man. ('At least he knows it's a person,' my friend said. 'The one

I'm sleeping with probably thinks Greer is a type of cheese.')

Then a man tried to kill me. He put his hands around my neck, and he tried to squeeze the breath and the life from me, and when he did that, he ruptured my mind and transformed me into a frightened creature, a wild thing on the run that either cowers or lashes out when threatened.

My need for the safety of home is part of the reason that we are still here, in this crumbling rented flat, though we have talked about moving many, many times. After my attack, the streets no longer felt safe. I couldn't go back to the house I'd been sharing with friends without being reminded of the feeling of lying on the pavement with a man's hands around my neck while the other men turned their backs and walked away, so casually. Besides, the other men were still out there, I assumed in the area; only my assailant had been arrested. So I had to move.

After a stint with my grandmother and a few months in an attic flat above a pub theatre shared with my friend Holly and a frequently stoned actor in his sixties who had written a bestselling novel in the eighties about crack addiction in the projects, and who threatened gentlemen callers with 'New York justice' if they did anything to hurt either of us – a hedonistic, joyfully unconventional time in my life – I found this place. And in it was a kind man who did not deserve my rage or my fear. A man who would keep me safe.

When the PTSD was at its worst, I thought I might end up alone. I still do, in my lowest moments. When the fury gripped me, it was like succumbing to a sickness. My whole body would be humming with it.

I read once that people with PTSD were incapable of experiencing love. 'Looks like we beat the odds,' I joked, to my husband, not long after we married. I don't believe this theory is true. But I have found that sometimes, especially when I feel the familiar symptoms resurrecting themselves, I get the sudden urge to bolt. How else to put it? It feels like it might be easier to be alone, to have to take care only of myself. It feels like I do not deserve love.

While I was living with my grandmother, she showed me the tin box in which she keeps old documents (women, she often says, are the keepers and transmitters of a family's history). On my great-grandmother's marriage certificate, I read the word 'spinster' and laughed. How quaint and old-fashioned it seemed. Not to mention unfair. Her new husband had been, before marriage, a 'bachelor', which hardly had the same connotations.

In the cultural imagination, spinsters are older women who have been 'left on the shelf'. Historically, these women were women who spun for a living, but the word's meaning shifted to connote any woman who was poor or unmarried. These women, I suppose, sometimes also kept cats. Often, when people speak of 'crazy cat ladies', there is contained within the archetype an implication that, for these women, their cats are surrogate children into which they channel their displaced maternal instincts. There is something unnatural about this. These women, we are told, exude sadness and desperation.

'I'm not saying that I need something to channel my frustrated maternal instincts into,' I say to my husband, tears streaming down my face, 'but wouldn't it be nice to just, you know, have a little thing to look after during this terrible time? To have something to focus on other than ourselves and the fact that we are stuck in this flat while a terrifying disease rages outside?'

For the first time in years, we have found ourselves without a flatmate. With the pandemic underway, we are under no pressure to get another. The souls of the downstairs and upstairs cats have departed this plane, with the upstairs cat, fittingly, dispatched to kitty heaven and the downstairs cat . . . well . . . the mean part of me would say that where he is now is pretty toasty for him in his little fur coat. A new kitten would have no adversaries.

My husband is running out of reasons to say no.

Besides, I have consulted the internet for backup. I ask people to tell me the best thing about having a cat. A lot of people say that having a cat means you laugh a lot.

'They are super haughty but also total derps,' one says. 'Mine likes to floss his teeth on the blind cords and suck his own nipples,' replies another. 'The best thing is that feeling of total submission to a higher power,' I am told by a third, possibly of the sadomasochist persuasion, who left me mildly concerned for his welfare.

These are all convincing arguments, especially because, what with the deadly virus, we could really do with some levity around the place.

'What if we want to go on holiday?' my husband says. We are on about day five of my let's-get-a-kitten campaign and he is beginning to weaken.

'We're in the middle of a lockdown. We're not going anywhere.'

Unfortunately, it seems everyone else has had the same idea at the same time. Kittens appear and disappear from the listings within seconds, despite the – often suspicious-looking – sellers demanding hundreds of pounds. You're not supposed to leave a kitten alone for more than an hour or two, but that has ceased to be an issue for the many people now working from home.

I look into adopting a kitten from a charity, but their list of demands is impossible – if they are placing at all, which many are not. Not only do they want to inspect our home (via Zoom), and interview us, presumably to make sure that we aren't kitten-disembowelling Satanists (bad) or dog-owners (worse), they also want a letter from our landlords. It took two years to get them to fix the hole in our bedroom ceiling, so obtaining such a letter would be a bureaucratic nightmare I am not prepared to face (especially as, lamentably, the landlords' on-hold music is 'Mr Bojangles', a mawkish song about an alcoholic tramp who dances for tips, as if to warn tenants: *If you complain too much, this could be you*).

'Don't get one from a charity', a colleague messages me, privately. 'One lady shouted at me because I didn't want to take a cat with cat AIDS.'

(*Why is it 'cat AIDS' and not just 'AIDS'?* I wonder. My mother-in-law says their cat, Scampie, has 'a touch of cat dementia'. 'You can just say dementia, Mum,' my husband says.)

'I mean, it's £700 for just an average-looking cat.' I am reading listings out to my father on the telephone. 'In fact, it's a bit cock-eyed.'

'No one pays for cats around here,' my dad says. He lives in the countryside, where kittens are routinely put in sacks and thrown into the river. He alludes to this in his typical sardonic fashion, and I find myself laughing despite the darkness of the subject matter. My conversations with my dad are often like this: he never fails to make me hoot.

'Maybe this is my racket,' I say. 'Like all the black marketeers during the Blitz. I will make my coronavirus fortune by liberating Welsh kittens from certain death and transporting them to the homes of the metropolitan bourgeoisie.'

'It sounds like a lot of work,' my dad says. 'And you can't drive.'

Maybe, I think, it is women like me who are buying up all the kittens. Women who have unexpectedly found themselves with time on their hands. All my friends had plans for this year. Some were getting married, some were going travelling, some were excelling in their careers, or about to throw themselves back on to the singles market with renewed vigour. A few wanted to start trying for a baby. Now we all found ourselves at a loose end. Ella Masons in waiting. The crazy cat ladies of the future.

When you think about it, to call a childless woman a crazy cat lady is a fine way in which to neutralise a threat. 'There is something threatening about a woman who is not occupied with children,' writes Sheila Heti in *Motherhood*. 'There is something at-loose-ends feeling about such a woman. What is she going to do instead? What sort of trouble will she make?'

'I'm not sure I want children,' I used to say in my midtwenties, though what I really meant was that I had always wanted children, but was not sure how I could make it work when my life, career, and mind all felt so unstable. *I feel like every child is a book I will not write*, I used to think, though what I really meant was that I was sad that society wasn't set up in a way that would allow me to fully pursue my creative ambitions while also raising a child. 'I could live a perfectly happy life without children,' I used to say, though what I really meant was that I could learn to live with the pain.

On the morning of my sixth birthday, Molly had kittens. She had four: two girls, one black and one black-and-white, and two boys, one tabby, one ginger. I will never forget coming downstairs and peering into the cardboard box at these blind little creatures. They looked like tiny, pink, bald moles.

Aside from a trip to Disneyland, there is nothing more exciting to a six-year-old than a boxful of kittens, but my mother, who was nursing my two-week-old brother at the time, was less enthused. 'I walked into the living room once to try and find a place to sit down where I could feed your brother,' she told me. 'But there was a cat on every chair.'

'I've already done enough caring in my life,' I used to say, though really what I meant was that I had got used to the particular freedom of not being needed.

I have always seen the appeal of being a woman who looks after no one but herself. There's something exciting about the thought of being such a figure.

It is a fantasy that several other women I know – all writers – have confessed to me. Caring for others interferes with the work, we are told; our futures as women who write are haunted by the proverbial pram in the hall, the 'enemy' of good art. And it is true that art requires a certain degree of solitude, which many would call selfishness when it is claimed by a woman. I can sometimes be difficult to reach, so immersed am I in my own head, engaged in the act of writing even when I am not putting pen to paper or fingers to keyboard. It is also an uncomfortable fact that many children bore me; that in a family setting I often cannot help but open a newspaper, in the manner of a retro, archetypal father. (At an exhibition about masculinity, the work that hit me the most was a photograph of a man concealed by a gigantic broadsheet newspaper. I felt a surge of love, as though my own father was in the room.)

I was a 'child carer', but for many years, I never identified with that term; I felt maybe that it located my childhood as a site of pity, and that's not how I felt about it at all. My brother has severe autism, and it brought enormous challenges, but when I think about my childhood, what I mostly feel is gratitude. When parents talk about the love they have for their children being unlike any other, I can empathise a little. I am childless (at times, even recently, I have considered myself 'child-free', an important alternative, but as I write this, I feel child-less), and I have known a love so big that you are unsure where to put it all. It's like sensory overload: intense and terrifying, almost like grief. There are times when I'm not sure I could take a love that big again, that it would come to dominate all the space that lies within me for the work of writing, just as my brother dominated our chaotic, loving home.

He was not like other babies, but I didn't notice; I was a child. But I do remember how beautiful he was: everybody does. He stopped people in their tracks. Even now, when I look at photographs of him, I am struck by those huge blue eyes. Sometimes they are focused on the camera, but often they are not. They gaze off towards some distant point behind you, unknowable.

~

In the end, I find the woman with the kittens on Twitter. Or rather, I find Carin, who got her cats from the same woman and puts us in touch.

I tell my husband that, as a treat, he can choose which kitten we take home. He is still unsure, but his resistance is crumbling. By this point, he'll do anything as long as I stop talking.

Then one day, when we are leaving the house for our government-mandated walk around the neighbourhood, we see a rat in the front garden. It is large, and brown, and it disappears through a crack under the stone steps when we become aware of its presence, its tail curling and flicking behind it like a worm. We both shudder.

'It's unlikely to come upstairs,' I say, 'if we have a cat.'

We study the first video we are sent, adjusting the volume as the high-pitched mews blast from my phone speaker. The kittens don't stay still long enough to get a good look, so we have to keep pausing. My husband likes the tortoise-shell one with the flash of white on its bib and forehead. There's a tiny white tip on her pointy little tail, too, and she is wearing white ankle socks. She's the sweetest kitten that I have ever seen, and I fall immediately in love.

The kitten's mother has rejected her, so provided she is able to eat solids, she will be ready for her new home on Saturday. There is also, I am told, an adult cat in residence that 'isn't getting along' with the kittens. I know what this means from listening to friends talk about their flatmates. They say, 'We just haven't clicked,' but what they really mean is, 'She put all the washing-up in my bed while I was away at a family funeral because I refused to join the ayahuasca orgy she was hosting.' It means: *they need to go, and soon.*

All the same, I try not to get my hopes up. I have been disappointed before. No money is changing hands. Even when the day comes, I'm aware that spending over a hundred pounds on cat paraphernalia is no guarantee that things won't fall through.

I look on Google Maps to see where the woman lives.

It is out beyond the ring road that circles the city. As we are in a lockdown, and advised to avoid public transport, we will need to go on foot. It is an eleven-mile round trip.

We have bought a cat carrier from Amazon (my boycott of Amazon had been going really well until we adopted a kitten at short notice during a global pandemic) and we have lined it with a hand towel. 'In case she shits,' I say solemnly to my husband. It is a bright, fine day in May.

We have been wondering if it is possible to catch the virus from a cat. They think it came from a bat or a pangolin, so it's not the most unreasonable of questions. My husband looks it up online. '"Pet owners are urged to adopt good hygiene practices",' he reads. '"Including handwashing before and after being around or handling animals, their food, or supplies, as well as avoiding kissing them."

'No kissing?' he says. 'Let's call the whole thing off.'

We laugh at the idea that you'd kiss your cat. What kind of deranged person does that? Just two days later, as he 'puts her to bed', I will look through the door into the darkened living room and think I see him placing his lips gently against her furry forehead as he says goodnight.

Looking back on the year I was six, I wonder if the kittens distracted me from feeling displaced by my new baby brother; I don't recall ever being jealous of him, or feeling that I didn't get enough attention. The kittens were far more exciting than he was.

When they grew bigger, I was told that I was allowed to keep one. I wanted the little black kitten. I had already decided that I wanted to be a witch; in fact, I had been emitting strong goth vibes since toddlerdom, having caused a furore at my Christian nursery with my pet rubber skeleton, which I had named, in a sublime act of pre-internet trolling, Mary.

At my last school, my friend's religious mother had already taken my mother aside to say, 'Please get your daughter to stop playing witches with my daughter, because we actually believe in them and find them frightening.'

My mother duly told me that it was probably best if I didn't play witches with this particular little girl.

'Did you play with Jennifer today?' my mother asked, when she picked me up the following afternoon. I confirmed that I had.

'And what did you play?'

'Car crashes,' I said.

'Oh,' my mother said. 'And, er . . . were you the doctors that made people better?'

'No,' I said. 'We were the witches that made it happen.'

Which goes to show what happens when you try to ban things.

Yes, the black cat was the one for me. That was, until my friend, a girl with whom I was deeply competitive, said she wanted the black-and-white one. So I kept her instead, because I always want what I cannot have. We named her Jessie.

Witches, of course, were the original crazy cat ladies. Like Hecate, they were thought to keep familiars – animal spirits that aided them with their magic – most commonly black cats. It was even suggested that women could take feline form, prowling around at night only to bear the scars of their activities on their human bodies the next morning.

The evil demon Lilith of Hebrew mythology, the first wife of Adam and a strangler of children, was believed by Jews in Spain to be able to transform into La Broosha, a vampire cat that sucked the blood from infants. In Chinese folklore, cats were also associated with vampires, with pregnant or black cats having the mystical ability to reanimate corpses and turn them into bloodsucking '*jiangshi*'. In Japan, though the cat was venerated, there was also a belief in vampire cats, and their tails – believed to contain a cat's magic – were cut off in order to prevent them from becoming demons.

The medieval belief in witches being able to transform into cats, or of witches allowing cats to suck their blood or drinking the blood of infants, may have roots in these earlier mythologies. The marks that were left on women's bodies by the feeding of their familiars were known as witches' marks, and the act was portrayed as an uncanny, unnatural perversion of the idea of the breastfeeding mother.

It was with Christianity that the fear of the witch began to mount. According to the Jungian psychologist Marie-Louise von Franz, the black cat became the 'dark side' to the Mother of God; sterile as opposed to fertile, they were believed to mate with the devil, preventing pregnancy in humans and causing crops to fail. 'The whole devilish aspect of the cat, its witch aspect, has only come into the foreground since the time of Christianity. That has to do with the patriarchal banishing of the feminine shadow,' she writes.

Vox in Rama, issued by Pope Gregory IX in 1233, declared black cats an embodiment of Satan, paving the way for their persecution and torture, as well as encouraging the same treatment for their owners.

In the early modern period, thousands and thousands of people, most of them marginalised women and children, were executed following witch trials, the instigators of which claimed their victims worshipped the devil. Cats, too, were hanged, burned at the stake, thrown from the tops of bell towers and even, on the Isle of Mull, tortured on spits. Elizabeth I didn't consider it a party if there weren't a few cats set on fire.

The pre-Christian beliefs of these wise women, or 'herb-mothers', with their herbalism and reverence for nature and animals, saw them perceived as a threat to the medieval church. Whether young or old, a woman who kept cats was worthy of suspicion. If she was old, single, and childless, then she was a haggard, barren, evil old crone, and any herbalist wisdom she possessed was not early medicine, but magic.

If she was young and attractive, then her sexuality was used against her: she was as loose and wanton as a cat in heat, suckling demons and imps, perhaps even mating with the devil himself.

It is significant that familiars were considered by some occultists to be a projection of the witch-owner's personality: a double, or alter ego. That those familiars were so often cats is also something I find particularly interesting. Though mostly domesticated, a cat, unlike a dog, always keeps a part of herself back. She is mysterious and ungovernable. Stubbornly autonomous, she refuses to take orders. While humans sleep, she disappears into the night with slinky diso-bedience, and gets up to god-knows-what with god-knows-who. She is cunning, clever, and worst of all, slutty with it. Such qualities are enough, in a cat, to arouse suspicion. In a woman, they are unforgivable, and must be punished.

A witch, Madeline Miller writes, is a woman who has too much power.

I once read an article in which an animal charity claims that black cats are not being adopted because they don't look as good in photographs that are posted to social media, as their features don't stand out as much. One London shelter said it received thirty telephone calls about a tabby kitten that they advertised on their Facebook page; the black kittens posted for rehoming on the same day received just one enquiry. This is despite the fact that, in Britain, unlike in other countries, black cats are mostly considered lucky, perhaps owing to their sacredness in Celtic mythology. (In one old Welsh rhyme, a black cat is said to keep fever from the door of a family home.)

During the first lockdown, my friend Holly, the one who accumulates cats, acquires a new one. Her New York roommate has moved in with his highly allergic girlfriend, and leaves behind a beautiful black cat named Nelson. Holly tells me that the cat shelters in America are full of black cats, not because of Instagram, but because some people can be so religious and superstitious that they do not want a devilish animal in their house.

Holly and her boyfriend share a one-bedroom apartment in Brooklyn, and Nelson is not small by any means. But Holly has never allowed a slightly inconvenient, poky living situation to stop her from pursuing her dreams of cat ownership. In this way, she is truly inspirational.

I text my friend Shakes about the kitten I have found online. She lives on the other side of the country and is working all hours as a doctor. 'I think we are going to get a cat,' I say.

Shakes's cat, like Felix, Holly's cat in Britain, is a ragdoll, except Shakes's cat is white. He is the most quintessential Bond-villain cat I have ever seen. The campest of cats, for the campest of women: Shakes has the personality of a drag queen in a curvaceous Egyptian anaesthetist's body.

Her cat's name is Barney, but online he operates under the moniker 'Professor Meow Meow'. I don't know how much he cost, but it looks like a lot. This is the woman who put her first instalment of 'ash cash' (a payment received by medical professionals for signing a cremation certificate) towards a leopard-print fur coat and a pair of Christian Louboutin shoes.

'What breed is she?' Shakes asks. I imagine her squinting at the grainy screenshot of my kitten while on a break from intubating Covid patients.

'Fuck knows,' I type. 'All of them?'

Because of social distancing, and because the woman with the kittens is in the middle of Eid celebrations with her family, the transfer of the kitten takes mere seconds.

'Do you want to come and see the others?' she asks, ever-hopeful that we will take a sibling, too.

'Better not,' we say. I have pushed my luck far enough already, and my husband knows I'll try and take them all home given half the chance.

'Hello, darling,' I say to the tiny, mewing, teacup-sized creature that is placed into our hands and then transferred into the cat carrier. She is frightened, and confused, and she wants her mother. I know instantly that I will do anything for her.

'Don't take our kitten!' the woman's children protest. I know how they feel. I've been there myself.

'Don't worry,' I say. 'I promise we'll look after her and make her the happiest kitten in the entire world. She will be so loved.'

I am using my special talking-to-children voice. They are unimpressed. But I mean it. She is ours. Or, rather: we are hers.

Before the pandemic, I think I had low life-esteem. There were certain things that I had come to expect from adulthood, such as perhaps one day owning my own home, but things hadn't happened that way. I had found a man I loved and my career as a writer was going well enough, and for that I was grateful. It had seemed doubtful that we would stop renting anytime soon, however – we shared with other people in order to save towards a house, and in hindsight we were incredibly lucky that we never ended up with anyone truly unhinged. But nonetheless, my life felt makeshift, temporary. I was always looking ahead to someplace in the future: a stable set-up, a place that was mine.

Those traditional markers of adulthood – a house, children, stability – can feel quite out of reach when you have a chain-smoking Kiwi in the spare room and a guitar-shredding Italian on the floor in the living room. To this day, my husband insists that, a few years back, we sublet a room to an antipodean couple who were spending a few weeks in the city. Such arrangements were not unheard of – Holly had even lived in the airing cupboard for a couple of months when she got her first job – but I genuinely have no memory of these apparently very nice people with whom I am told I shared my home. Such was the unstable life of a twenty-something renter: it was a perpetual carousel of flatmates.

(Also, I smoked a fair bit of weed and my memory wasn't all that great.)

I didn't dislike my life then, and I wasn't unhappy. I loved living with other people, loved the hilarious camaraderie of getting drunk at the kitchen table, the in-jokes and the shared history. It felt as though we were all in the same boat, all pitching and rolling on the rough seas of our twenties. The questions of marriage and children and home ownership lurked in the background like a poltergeist plotting to ruin a cocktail party, but we had time – didn't we?

Then, a strange thing started happening in my mid-to-late twenties: money started appearing. Suddenly, peers who had always been complaining about being hard-up came into possession of two-bed Victorian flats in 'up and coming' (read: gentrifying) areas. Inheritances were inherited, trust funds were unlocked, paintings were sold, and deposits were summoned. Photographs of keys were uploaded with excited captions; the Farrow & Ball paint came out; social media became a daily renovations diary, and my peers started talking about tradespeople using proprietorial language (saying 'my carpenter' is, I maintain, a sure sign of a twat).

And good for them, I thought, while privately also thinking that anyone showing off property online in the middle of a housing crisis should also have to caption it with an itemised list of which lump sums came from which sources ('£50k from Granny, and £70k from the account in Monaco that Daddy set up during the last financial crisis, and another £20k from Mummy's stolen Nazi vase').

It wasn't the politics of envy I was experiencing so much as the politics of 'waking up every time it rains heavily because you're still traumatised from the leak in your bedroom that took your landlord two years to repair'.

A stable life, a place of our own, became the holy grail. But in desiring it, I never looked around at what I had.

Then the pandemic hit and, for the first time in years, it was just the two of us, with no pressure to fill the spare room. I looked around the shabby flat and, beyond the hideous woodchip wallpaper and scuffed skirting boards, I was surprised to find a life. Not some inadequate, ephemeral, ersatz life made bearable by the thought of some stable, glittering future in a home we'd one day own, but an actual life, one that I was living right now. A life with a husband and a history and furniture, and roses that I had grown myself.

Crises have a tendency to do that to you – they make you take stock. And I found that all my particular inventory was lacking was a cat.

Perhaps being a writer was part of it. Writers and artists have always been drawn to cats, especially women writers and artists. Alice Walker wrote of her 'familiar' Frida (named after Frida Kahlo, who painted herself with an ominous-looking black cat on her shoulder): 'When it is bedtime I pick her up, cuddle her, whisper what a sweet creature she is, how beautiful and wonderful, how lucky I am to have her in my life, and that I will love her always.'

My tentativeness was possibly a question of not wanting to get hurt again. Having a cat makes you vulnerable – I had forgotten how, until we take our lockdown kitten home, and tales of sick or dying cats begin to get me in the gut. *Get a grip*, I think to myself, as I read Mary Gaitskill's tale of her 'Lost Cat' Gattino – a poor stray, half-blind kitten that she'd brought home from Italy – and find myself weeping at the thought of him desperate and alone and confused in the snow.

When Gaitskill lost Gattino, she was distraught. She looked for him for over a year. She consulted psychics, looked into the possibility of witchcraft. In other words, like a lot of people who are grieving, she turned to magical thinking.

And even if it is a cat, it is still grief. Her story recalls that of the Welsh artist Gwen John, who lost her cat Tiger in a French village where she had been painting with Rodin. You can see how much John loved cats from looking at her paintings: two of her portraits (1918–22's *Girl With Cat* and 1920–25's *Young Woman Holding a Black Cat*) show a pale, attractive young woman holding a black cat in her arms. The woman looks profoundly sad as she stares into the middle distance beyond the canvas, a melancholia that you can't help but project on to John, who was so unhappy in love. She also produced paintings of her calico cat Edgar Quinet, rendered with tender affection.

When Tiger went missing, John went from house to house searching, and was mocked for it, though this didn't prevent her from continuing to look. She slept outside while waiting for him to come back. Was she a crazy cat lady, or simply a person who had lost a friend for whom she cared deeply, and at a time when she was being driven mad by unrequited love?

For Gaitskill, losing her cat had left her open to examine all the other forms of love in her life, all those that had left her feeling rejected, and wanting. For Gaitskill, 'a lost, hungry little animal dying as it tries to find its way back home in the cold' is a metaphor for love.

These stories of lost cats, recalling as they do my own beloved Molly, make me cry. Of course, I am crying at all sorts of things these days. I cry at the death tolls in the news, and from fear for the vulnerable. I cry because, in lockdown, I am making so few new memories that my brain starts replaying old ones, and long-banished sadnesses and regrets return to tug at me in the small hours. I cry for my mother, who is a force to be reckoned with, but who is also poor, and alone, and likely to become more so. I cry because I am frightened for Shakes, who is on the frontline helping to save lives, and who is more at risk because of her job and her ethnicity. I cry at my doctor aunt's email to the family, which sounds as though she is going into battle:

We will continue working until we get ill. Hopefully not all GPs and ANPs will be ill at the same time. Despite the challenges, I have never regretted my career choice.

Mum and Dad are often in my thoughts, and I am sure Dad would have views on how this is all being handled. Mum would be afraid, I think, so I am relieved that she is not here to witness it.

I cry because my brother is in a care home hundreds of miles away, and I don't know when I will see his face and get to hold him. I cry because I think I want to have a baby, and the world has turned so dark so quickly that I can no longer envisage that decision not being wrought with terror. I cry with fear and with rage and with pity.

~

Amid the pain, there are moments of deep relief: the silence, the deadness of time and space, feels like a respite. It's an astonishingly bright spring. In the evenings, after we have finished working, we sit on the front step and listen to the parrots singing in the trees. We have concocted a cocktail, which I call the honeymoon margarita, consisting of the limoncello we brought back from Ischia, ice-cold from the freezer and shaken with sugar, tequila, lemon juice. (The lemons that hang from the trees in the bay of Naples are the size of large kittens, and I spent that blissful trip in a lemon-patterned sundress and a large, white straw hat, intoxicated with happiness.)

In several months' time, I will need three fillings in my teeth, but for now: alcohol helps.

~

There's a hierarchy of grief; of course there is. A seven-year-old whose little tortoiseshell cat Molly has wandered off after a house move will experience grief, but not to the same extent that she will in a decade's time, when her grandmother dies in hospital, or that she will several years after that, when her grandfather dies suddenly (he was a microbiologist and a doctor who worked with children with cystic fibrosis, and yes, as my aunt noted, he certainly would have had views about how all this is being handled). But it's still, on some level, grief.

As Gaitskill writes: 'Who decides which relationships are appropriate and which are not? Which deaths are tragic and which are not? Who decides what is big and what is little?'

My friend Sarah once told me a story that I think about often. At the time, we were working at the same newspaper, and she was writing about the refugee camp in Calais that is sometimes ignorantly referred to as 'the Jungle'. She had gone to the camp to speak to refugees who were living there, and was in the process of interviewing a man named Akeel who had experienced more suffering than most of us will face in our lifetimes. He had fled Isis in Iraq, and then taken the long, arduous, dangerous journey across land and sea to reach Calais, where he had been for six months, living in a tent and eating food out of cans. He was twenty-eight, the same age as Sarah.

As Akeel talked, Sarah felt her phone vibrate in her pocket. She ignored it, and eventually it stopped. A minute or so later, it started to vibrate again. Akeel stopped talking and asked if she wanted to take the call, but Sarah said no, apologising for the disruption. It rang again, and again she ignored it. But when it rang the fourth time, she realised that something must have happened. She looked at the screen and saw that it was her father who had been calling. 'I'd better take this,' she said.

When she answered, her father was crying, and Sarah walked away from the makeshift tarpaulin-roofed structure she and Akeel were in, in order to have some privacy in which to process what she anticipated was going to be some extremely traumatic news. 'What's happened?' she asked, fearing the worst.

'It's Susie,' said her dad. 'She was in the garden under her favourite bush. I found her this morning. She's dead.'

Susie was the family cat, and Sarah's dad was crying more than she had ever heard him cry before.

As anyone who has seen or heard their father in such a state will know, it is almost impossible not to cry when your dad is crying. But Sarah is a professional, so she ended the call and wiped her eyes and went back to her interview with Akeel.

'What's wrong?' Akeel asked, when Sarah sat back down. *Oh, God*, Sarah thought. *I can't tell him why I look so upset.* In the face of this man's suffering, a dead cat seemed so trivial, and to weep for one while standing in the middle of a place like this seemed tactless and embarrassing. She felt her privilege acutely, and brushed him off.

But Akeel kept asking, and Sarah kept refusing to say. Eventually, the awkwardness at withholding what had happened became too much.

'It's Susie, the cat,' she told Akeel. 'My dad was crying because he found her dead this morning. It's silly.'

She was mortified, but Akeel reached out and put his hand on her arm. 'It's not silly,' he said. 'When my cat died, in Baghdad, I cried. Tell me . . . do you still live at home with your father?'

Sarah said no, she didn't; that her parents were divorced and that she and her sister had long left home.

'That cat,' said Akeel, 'was probably the last remnant your dad had of his family.'

The kitten meows unceasingly as we walk through the meandering north London suburbs. We hold the carrier up to our faces and offer soothing words, already adopting the 'cat voices' that we will come to use daily in our inter-actions with her. 'It'll be OK, little cat,' we say. 'Don't worry, you're safe.'

She is clearly in a state of fear and distress at being taken from the familiar smells of home and the warmth of her family, and then, to make things worse, the heavens open just as we are entering the large, green expanse of the Heath. The cat carrier is not entirely waterproof, espe-cially not in a downpour such as this, so I place my anorak over it, and we rush towards a dry bench nestled beneath some thick trees. We sit eating the sandwiches we have packed, watching the rain, while the kitten falls asleep in the case next to us. And despite the terror of the news and the lockdown and the fact that I am still processing this major world event that has changed everything, I feel happy. There are three of us. We have become a weird little family, of sorts.

II

Summer

It's late summer and I am sitting in a Greek taverna oppo-site my husband, crying into my octopus *stifado*. The reason that I am crying is because of a cat. It is also because I have drunk two frozen margaritas on an empty stomach, in other words, I am tipsy enough that I am seriously considering asking the waiter if he knows where we can 'get some weed'. Alcohol is definitely a factor in my tears. So is the stress of embarking upon possibly ill-advised international travel during a global crisis. Nevertheless, the cat is what sets me off.

The cat has a limp, you see. She lollops from table to table, clearly in pain, emitting the occasional agonised mew. And for some reason, despite being habituated to the sight of scrawny, neglected Greek cats, this hits me in the heart. Since bringing home our lockdown kitten, the plight of cats has begun to affect me emotionally as it never has before.

I am not an animal lover, especially. Until my parents got divorced, I was raised vegetarian (it was when my mother started buying ham that I clocked that their marriage might be over), but after that I became an indiscriminate carnivore. I ate all manner of horrible, delicious, unethical things, espe-cially while living in France: a sausage made from pig's anus, duck tongue salad, bone marrow stuffed with caviar, foie gras.

Even as I cry over the cat, I am sitting with the remains of an incredible sentient being before me, swimming not in the sea where he belonged, but in a delectable red wine sauce. I have felt guilty about the consumption of octopodes (I am pretentious, therefore prefer the Greek plural) since reading a vivid description written by the novelist Ben Lerner, but as well as making me emotional, the drink has also affected my morals.

My husband sits in front of me as I sob. He is not merely irritated. He is infuriated. I sympathise: when a woman sits opposite a man in a restaurant and that woman is in tears, the natural conclusion drawn by everyone in the vicinity is that the man – who is obviously a cad and a scoundrel – is the reason. His reputation among the Greek people has already been tarnished from a previous holiday, when a mosquito bite to my eyelid resulted in a large swelling and the false assumption that he was a wife beater, leading to a menacing atmosphere wherever we went. This time, people are clearly staring.

The fact that I am crying about a cat adds insult to injury. I realise that he thinks I am insane, and yet I simply cannot stop. In the space of a summer, I've become a crazy cat lady, and I'm not sure how it happened.

The first sign comes in May, not long after we bring the kitten home.

I have bought a bottle and some kitten milk just in case, and it turns out this was a wise move. I crouch down to kitten-height and feed her from the bottle, learning to squeeze it just the right amount to keep the warm milk flowing in between the sharp edges of her teeth. I feed her until she turns her head away, and then I carry her through into the living room and set her down. She sleeps, wedged in between my leg and the arm of the sofa, as I try to turn the pages of my book quietly so as not to wake her.

Every morning, we open the door to the living room to be met by an extremely happy animal. She immediately approaches us for strokes, before spinning around. 'The kitten will present you with her anus for inspection,' my husband, who has become increasingly interested in cat behaviour and has been researching it online, reads aloud, the first time she does this. 'Charming.'

There is a particular blanket on my bed that she loves. After we have let her through, she comes in and kneads it with her little paws, purring like the motor in an electric toothbrush, her pointy tail in the air. I decide to buy her another, for the sofa, so she can snuggle up to it all night long, but it turns out that they have been discontinued.

After much searching online, I locate a second-hand blanket several miles north, and so I set out on foot to collect it (we are still being advised to avoid public transport). An errand like this is not how I would ever have chosen to spend my time before, but it seems that my devotion to this cat knows no bounds. Since the pandemic, my world has contracted, but it's more than that – I want to do everything I can to make her happy, even walking for miles, even when it gives me blisters.

'We must serve our fluffy overlords,' my father always says of the feline population. He is of the opinion that cats already secretly rule the world, and that most humans are simply too stupid to realise it. A subscriber to the toxoplasmosis theory, he believes that the parasite with which cats infect their human owners (or servants, as they come to be known) actually changes our brains to make us more amenable to cats. In other words, owning a cat turns us into cat lovers.

There is some scientific merit to this, and certainly anecdotally I have seen people who previously showed no interest in cats, and even an active dislike for them, become besotted with their own. (I have noted a similar phenomenon with children.)

Certainly since becoming a cat owner, I now notice other cats much more than I did before. On our daily walks, we have come to know the various neighbourhood cats, stopping to greet them like old friends. There's the magnificent amber-eyed tabby, who sits imperiously on the wall in front of his house, and the friendly black cat, who always likes to be stroked. I'd never noticed either of these cats before the kitten came into our lives.

Every time I speak to my father on the phone, he likes to update me as to the movements and activities of his two cats. I love my dad very much, but before I had my own cat, I will admit I did question why he thought I would be interested in yet another anecdote about having to remove a partially gnawed vole from his shoe. Now, though, I lap it up like it's celebrity gossip.

I decide that my taverna outburst is payback for the infamous Greek holiday incident of 2014, when, in a crowded restaurant, my husband insisted on feeding scraps of his meal to a nearby cat, contrary to all of my advice. The moment he dropped the piece of meat on the floor, a dozen other cats converged upon it, seemingly from nowhere, surrounding our table and drawing the attention of everyone else in the restaurant, because who isn't going to be visually drawn to the spectacle of a herd of cats surrounding an increasingly pink-faced Englishman? It was when one of the cats started bleeding from her vagina all over the floor that I could no longer contain myself.

'This is the best moment of my life,' I said.

I always knew, objectively, that people loved their cats to an unhinged degree. A cat was the reason that my best friend lived in a palatial central London apartment. This apartment was in an art deco building, which not only boasted a doorman – a rarity in this country – but also the largest roof garden in the city (so big that residents could run circuits of it for their daily exercise). The cat who lived in the apartment was a black cat belonging to a German banker who hardly spent any time in the city. My friend's job was to keep the cat in the manner to which he had become accustomed. In other words, her entire living situation had come about as a result of just how much this man cared about his cat.

Does that seem mad to you? It did to me. But now I have come to understand it.

Even when I was sane, I understood that some men like to tell women that they are not.

I'm trying to remember how old I was when a boy first told me I was crazy. One ex called me some other things – most notably a slut, while throwing a drink in my face, parking his tank firmly on my histrionic lawn in a display of drama so intense that I was forced to be witheringly calm in the face of it. But he never called me crazy. My Parisian ex did, because I can remember how he used to say it in French – *t'es folle!* This, from a man who had to be forcibly removed from the fun house at the Tuileries fairground during a magic mushroom trip. He had been in there for two hours, and was scaring the children. People in glass houses, or, as they say in France: *C'est l'hôpital qui se moque de la charité.*

By the time I reached my mid-twenties, I had become a writer, and being as I was also a woman, I was familiar enough with the historical patriarchal notion that all women are batshit hysterics with wandering wombs that must be cured through medicinal fingering to see its remnants in much of the correspondence I received from men. There's something about being accused of madness for writing something as objectionably anodyne as the suggestion that not all women like having their backsides groped by semi-erect strangers on public transport that makes you wonder if maybe you're not the one in the equation who is in dire need of professional help.

It was unpleasant, but at least the harassment remained in the online realm. I'll never forget a colleague telling me that a male reader had once recognised her while she was standing in front of the counter in the bank, and decided that this was the correct moment to tell her that she was 'too ugly to rape'.

'Oh love, you're not,' the female bank teller reassured her, in a cooing, comforting voice.

The internet men who called me crazy didn't matter to me; they were just words on a screen. Two years previously, a proper doctor had confirmed my madness, anyway.

'You're crazy, you're a psycho, you're unstable,' the men say. Even when it is the men who have made us that way.

When I first moved into my flat, it was only a few months after my near-death on a pavement with a man's hands around my neck. I was suffering episodes of depersonalisation, flashbacks, nightmares, rage, terror, panic, depression. I was scared to go out once night fell, and used to drink for courage. (Because I was a student, everyone else drank, too, so it wasn't until later that I came to understand how people with PTSD self-medicate with alcohol.) Outwardly, though, I was mostly functioning. I would carry on going to therapy, get better, graduate.

Nor did my erratic behaviour seem to turn off men. I spent a – blessedly brief – time internet dating. A couple of hours before one disastrous date, my friend K showed up on my doorstep with a bottle of wine in each hand. (She was having relationship problems. Our lives were one big relationship problem then.) By 6pm, we were humping the air to nineties hip hop. By 8pm, I was sitting on the carpet, saying, 'I cannot go on this date.' It wasn't just that I had had too much wine, it was also that, since my attack, I had stopped being sure of how to be a person. We concocted a plan: I would go to meet this man in the pub (he had already set off and I didn't want to stand him up); then I'd make my excuses, and we would reconvene at a bar to continue drinking.

Off I went to the pub, in no condition to be meeting anyone. I don't remember much of the date, except that I seemed to spend a fair part of it on the phone to K, and that whenever I banged my hand on the table for emphasis (which seemed to be a lot) the table would wobble, and both our drinks would spill. When my date – about whom I remember nothing now, except that he had black hair – kissed me, it felt wholly undeserved.

After my third or fourth phone call, the man got up to leave. *Fair enough,* I remember thinking blearily. *If I were on a date with me, I would leave too.* I completely respected his decision to ditch me. I spent most of my waking hours wanting to ditch myself. Clearly this man had something I lacked: self-esteem.

I finished my drink and ran home. I always used to run home in those days. I was terrified being on the street at night, and also, it was more efficient.

I was already home when I looked at my phone and saw a couple of missed calls and a message reading: 'Where are u?'

'You left, so I went home,' I replied.

'I went to the toilet,' he wrote back.

He had, it turned out, only been gone for a minute or two.

You would think this would be a dealbreaker, but apparently not. Despite my frankly insane behaviour, this man continued messaging me, calling me a 'hot mess' and asking how my thesis was going. I couldn't believe it. Naturally, the fact that this man was willing to lower himself to dating me made me not want to date him.

It might be that men will forgive a lot when a woman is

young and attractive enough in their eyes; when she reaches childbearing age and shows signs of madness, however, she takes on what they see as a tinge of desperation, becoming a figure of pity. Furthermore, I knew even then that some men sought out vulnerable women, seeing their fragile mental health as an asset that made them more malleable, riper for emotional manipulation.

Maybe I hid the madness well, but another man, at least, was able to see the good in me. By the summer, my flat-mate and I were together.

As the virus spreads and it becomes clear that our global state of emergency is not to be temporary, we are told to harvest the things that we are thankful for, blessings with which we can stuff our cheeks to get us through this long period of hibernation. I make a list: the part at the end of 'A Foggy Day' where Billie Holiday sings that the sun is shining upside down, and her voice blazes and jumps like light hitting a mirror; cutting a slice of cheese with a knife that's been used to chop garlic; dancing in the kitchen; a cold, cold martini when it's not quite evening; the smell of lilac.

Like everyone, I am frightened. But I am also thankful that this has happened now, and not during my second period of PTSD, after the Paris attacks, when I was in the grip of an anxiety so extreme that I could hardly leave the house – except to go to the doctor with a constellation of symptoms all of which coalesced to form a galaxy that spelled 'You're dying'. I wasn't dying, of course. I was traumatised, and my limbic system was on the prowl for an explanation. I became convinced that the world was conspiring to kill me in a thousand diverse and irrational ways, from a bomb on a bus to terminal cancer, via a plane falling from the sky and liver failure from drinking too many negronis. These fears were irrational, and seem so now when I write this in retrospect, but at the time they felt so present, so real.

My threat responses, which reside in the brain's amygdala, were hyperactive. When I was attacked in London, and fearing for my life in Paris, my hippocampus, which stores memories and is responsible for helping us sort the past from the present, was damaged; the past would not stay where it belonged. As a result, the fear associated with the trauma was constantly recurring, the experience elbowing its way into my everyday life, ever-present, that same cascade of chemicals reverberating again, and again.

For a deadly virus and a lockdown to enter this mix at that time would have been a disaster. As it was, it was several years on, so I greeted the news with cheery stoicism. Anxiety can do that to you, sometimes. You become such a catastrophist that when a catastrophe actually happens, you feel a surprising calm. You're ready for it.

One trauma therapist – Dr S, whom I saw after the

terrorist attacks – asked me for detailed worst-case scenarios, and after each sketched-out calamity (a bomb, a plane crash, everyone I love dying) she would say, with detached curiosity: 'Then what?' In this way, I talked myself out, my increasingly far-fetched doom fantasies becoming all the more ridiculous, until it became like a mantra, a way of directing a narrative until it ultimately ceased to bear any relationship to reality.

Then what?
Then what?
Then what?

'I'm too mad to have a baby,' I used to think. In this respect, I was correct.

Let me tell you about the cat I disliked, the cat that lived, until a couple of years ago, downstairs. I'm ashamed to say that I really hated this cat. It had a mean face, and used to hiss at you when you walked past. It shat in the alleyway down the side of the house with such frequency that you had to dance *en pointe* to reach the garden unscathed.

The cat belonged to our downstairs neighbour, a woman who could have been anything between the age of thirty-five and fifty, a woman who, if you were being euphemistically kind, you would say had had 'a hard life'. She lived alone, apart from the cat, and if she had once had any children, I suspected that they had been removed from her by the care system, a system that may also have failed her. She mostly wore a stained dressing gown and slippers, and hardly went out unless it was to the pub. She didn't give us any trouble, not really, unless you count the tobacco and weed smoke that floated into our flat through the hole in her ceiling, along with the sound of her horrible boyfriend calling her a cunt. When I thought of her, I felt mostly sympathy, though I would be lying if I didn't also admit that sharing a building with her meant learning to live with a certain level of unease, which hung in the air like the fumes from the rubbish they burned in her backyard on warm days. There existed in the building the potential for outbreaks of anger and even violence; it had happened before.

Sometimes, in life, you meet people who have been so extensively damaged that they no longer trust human beings at all. A bit like a rescue cat that has been so abused that she flinches each time you come near. You can try your best to be kind, but her faith has been so shaken that she is unable to see you as anything other than a moving, looming threat. A normal relationship will be extremely tricky, if not impossible. My downstairs neighbour was sometimes fearful, sometimes aggressive, always rude, occasionally unpleasant and constantly suspicious. You could engage her in conversation, but only in the most cursory of ways, so even asking about the cat was out of the question. To bring up the cat with her, even casually, would be seen as a criticism, even an attack. For that reason, we never found out the horrible cat's name. We knew him, when we referred to him at all, as Lisa's cat.

On the May morning we go to get the kitten, my husband wakes up set on a name.

'We will call her Mittens,' he says, authoritatively. I protest that Mittens is ridiculous, and he agrees. 'That is why,' he says, 'it must be her name.'

It is no joke, no triviality, a cat's name. Rather, it must be considered gravely, from all angles. A cat's name can have long-term repercussions, and I will tell you why.

When I was three, my mother left my father for a summer and moved back to the city, renting a room in a large Victorian house full of bohemians. Every evening, they would go outside into the garden and call the resident cat in for the night, as millions of cat owners have done throughout history, and will continue to do until the Earth dies, or cats inherit it, whichever is soonest.

My mother loved that house. It was looming and white, with stucco frills like a wedding cake. Each night a different person would cook for everyone else, usually something involving lentils. Everyone loved the house and its utopian division of labour. There was just one problem: the neighbours hated them.

'They were so friendly at first,' my mum's housemate said.

'A lovely Italian couple. We can't work out why they look at us with such disgust.'

My mother, too, was baffled by their stony unfriendliness. It wasn't until she learned of the cat's name, Catso, that she worked out the reason for their frosty relations.

'Hold on,' my mother said. 'Did you say *Catso*?'

My mother had lived in Italy for a year when she was eighteen and had had an Italian boyfriend named Maurizio, which, since we are discussing names, sounds so much sexier than Maurice. He had dropped out of university because he was so distracted by her beauty, and then my mother had gone back to England, leaving his academic career in tatters.

'Yes, Catso.'

'Well, no wonder they hate you.' My mother was crying with laughter.

'*Cazzo*', which sounds exactly like Catso, means penis in Italian. Except it's more vulgar than that, perhaps more like prick, or dickhead. It's used interchangeably with shit, and fuck. However you translate it, the neighbours won't have liked the people next door shouting it from their doorstep every evening into the still night air:

'SHIT! FUCK! PRICK!'

We discounted the usual suspects. Dictator names such as Chairman Miaow were overplayed. I had always claimed to want a cat called Tartarus, but that was when I hadn't known that we were having a girl. The writer Colette had a nice little line in cat names: Fanchette, Le Touteu, Minionne, Pinichette, and Petiteu were the real ones, and Kiki-La-Doucette and Saha were fictional. Though I appreciated the high camp in these names, they seemed a tad pretentious when used outside of France. In contrast, Doris Lessing's cat names were unappealingly utilitarian: Grey Cat, Black Cat.

I looked up the most popular cat names on the internet, but none of them really spoke to me (the most popular cat name, as of 2020 is, inexplicably, Oliver). The name I really wanted, Scampie, was already taken by my husband's parents' cat, the one who, at twenty, is suffering from 'a touch of cat dementia'. It was a shame, because it has become my belief that a cat should always be named after a foodstuff – and even better, a fish or a kind of seafood. I don't know why it's funny, it just is.

During our long journey home with the kitten, we traded ideas for names. My husband had taken one look at her and decided that she simply wasn't a Mittens, and so there was everything to play for. It was while brainstorming fish that I hit upon Mackerel. Mackerel is a rather unfashionable fish, but one that featured so often in the course of my childhood (OK, we were pescatarians, but we *said* we were vegetarians) that I wasn't able to eat it again until very recently.

A mackerel sky is a sky in which the clouds make an undulating rippling pattern, like the scales of a fish, or, for example, the tortoiseshell coat of a cat. There is a cat called Mackerel in Haruki Murakami's novel *The Wind-up Bird Chronicle* – Murakami himself once owned a cat by this name. I was ignorant of these facts, being neither a meteorologist nor a fan of Murakami, who I hope writes better cats than he does female characters – or, at the very least, doesn't mention their tits quite so much. No, we chose Mackerel as a name because she is, simply, a Mackerel. There was nothing to be done about it.

Of course, every cat owner knows that there is never just one name. T. S. Eliot writes that a cat has 'three different names', but even this seems too slight a number. A cat becomes a member of the family, and so over time, his or her name morphs into a hundred bastardisations and nicknames. And so she comes to not only be Mackerel, but to also be Mackerelcat, Little Mac, Big Mac, Pwdin (Welsh for pudding), Flopsy, Desert Rat, Squirrel, Hamcat, Baby Cat, Poo Cat, Poo Paws, Chaton, Macreauchaton, Chatonneuf-du-cat, and – while having to suffer the indignities of the vet's Elizabethan collar – Lady Mackerel Cattington. She greets all of these epithets with a resigned dignity that befits her status as the superior being.

When the upstairs cat was still alive, we named him Jimi, even though he already had a name; our neighbour called him Tiger. In many ways, Tiger suited him better – he was a beautiful, dignified Maine Coone tabby – but for some reason, when he entered our premises (which was often, as he was on a vegetarian diet, and aware of our potential as purveyors of ham), he became Jimi. I have since learned that it is considered poor form to feed another person's cat, especially when they are not supposed to be eating flesh, let alone to give that cat a new name. But strangely, it felt as though Jimi was as much our cat as anyone else's. Or, rather, he belonged to nobody. He came and went as he pleased, unwittingly mimicking the wave of flatmates, and when our upstairs neighbour was out and he waited patiently outside our cat-flap-less front door, it would have been a hard heart indeed who would have left him in the cold.

I loved Mackerel immediately, with the ferocity of a woman who had been craving a small thing to look after for a long time. I hesitate to buy into the 'baby substitute' theory, but it is true that I am a certain age. And it is true that, despite believing for many years that I wasn't sure I wanted to be a mother, that I had already spent too much of my life as a carer, the still, small voice was crying out for something to love.

In 'Double Negative', a micro-story that, in characteristic style, wryly summarises the questioning state in which I sometimes find myself, Lydia Davis writes: 'At a certain point in her life, she realises it is not so much that she wants to have a child as that she does not want not to have a child, or not to have had a child.'

To put it another way: I find myself wondering how much of my longing for a child is merely a desire to future-proof my life against possible regret.

'But you're a career woman,' my mother-in-law said, when I confessed this desire I have for a child. (No one, I have long remarked, ever uses the term 'career man'.)

This is a woman who has birthed and raised nine children, and as a result tends to be extremely wise in these matters.

'You can do both,' I said.

'Can you?' she said.

Really, my career has never been the issue, though it is true that the lack of stability that freelancing brings led me to push my desire to one side. When I think about it, though, it was my madness that stole several of my most fertile years, that made the notion of a child not merely unfeasible but potentially harmful, to any potential child, to myself, and to the man I loved.

I rarely think about the man who tried to strangle me to death when I was twenty-three, except to occasionally reflect on the chain of events that it set off. When I got into my pyjamas and dragged my bruised body beneath the covers that morning, sobbing as I waited for the arrival of both the police and my driving-through-the-night mother, I remember being struck by the thought that this man's violence would ricochet through my twenties in myriad, unforeseeable ways. The attack was over, but it also wasn't. It would play out for years to come, perhaps forever. The 'before' of my life had been brutalised; I now dwelled in an aftermath.

And so it proved.

From girlhood, we are imbued with the knowledge that a life-changing act of violence could be wrought against us. So this was mine.

Then what?
Then what?
Then what?

'What was your daughter doing out so late?' the policeman asked my mother. The dark velvet night should, after all, be left to the whores, the minxes, the strays.

She thought that she had seen my attack in the cards. She had seen things in the cards before: a friend's teenage pregnancy, dismissed at the time as a misreading, until the girl's belly began to swell. We are a witchy family: a great uncle had predicted his own death, or so the story goes.

He had been reading tarot for my grandmother and her friends. When one lad sat down and chose his cards, the man's face changed. He abruptly put the cards away and told everyone to go home. He later told my grandmother that he had seen the boy's death. He named the time and the place: it would be at the railway station. The news somehow got back to the boy, and he showed up a few days later to show them that he was still alive.

The house was full of flowers. It was the uncle who had dropped dead at the station, despite only being in his forties. He had not seen the boy's death in the cards, but his own.

After I was attacked, my mother got rid of her tarot cards. The card she had pulled in the reading that she had done for me was the Magician reversed, a card of madness and malice. In her distress at what had happened to me, she became concerned that she had opened up our lives to dark forces by messing with the tarot; that the knowledge it confers upon the reader must always be compensated for elsewhere. She said it was either that, or she simply wasn't very good at reading the cards, so it was best to stop.

'We meet our unconscious in our own destinies,' the terrible therapist said, attributing this maxim to Carl Jung. This was after the Paris attacks, but the terrible therapist – who happened to be a man and was, unlike my previous trauma therapist, private and paid for by my employer – seemed less interested in the real-life terrorist incident and its effects than in exploring the idea that I somehow subconsciously attracted male violence.

It sounded a lot like blame.

'Has it ever occurred to you,' I said to my mother, 'that perhaps it wasn't a case of him predicting his own death, but a self-fulfilling prophecy?'

'Go on . . .' she said.

'What if he was so frightened for this poor boy, whose death he believed he had forecast, and maybe even caused by toying with the supernatural, that he went to the train station to try and save him? Perhaps he was so terrified by what might happen that his own heart couldn't cope with the strain?'

My mother admitted that she had never thought of that.

My mother had a black cat, Dudu (pronounced 'Didi', a pun: '*du*' is Welsh for 'black'). Dudu had turned up one day during my childhood and refused to leave. At first, we had assumed he was another black cat, the one who had been stealing Jessie's food. This cat we called 'The Imposter' because, when you caught a glimpse of him out of the corner of your eye, you would simply assume that he was Jessie. This was an effective strategy. What The Imposter hadn't banked on, however, was having an imposter of his own.

Dudu was large and boxy, yet also panther-like. He was the sort of animal who, if glimpsed from extremely far away by someone with poor eyesight, might lead you to call your local newspaper with a big cat sighting. This proud, sleek demeanour was somewhat undercut by an ongoing dental issue that meant he dribbled constantly and left gooey white trails all over the sofa and cushions, which would dry and crust so they resembled, I hate to say it, the stains left by semen. But Dudu was never one to let something like that destroy his confidence.

I suspect he was a bit of a macho asshole, because Jessie's initial, quasi-maternal tolerance of him eventually morphed into loathing, and it was decided that she would go and live with my father, stepmother and youngest brother, where she would be left alone in peace.

~

Like stubbornly independent cats, women who lived alone were historically seen as disobedient. This made them a threat to the patriarchal order, as did their arcane knowledge of female reproduction, of how to prevent – and, if necessary, end – a pregnancy.

In *Caliban and the Witch*, Silvia Federici writes of how 'witch-hunting in Europe was an attack on women's resistance to the spread of capitalist relations and the power that women had gained by virtue of their sexuality, their control over reproduction, and their ability to heal'.

The female body was to be put to work. The 'magic' of these women was a form of resistance, insubordination, and even, Federici suggests, a refusal to perform this labour.

A single mother with a black cat, reading fortunes for the neighbourhood. They'd have definitely burned her as a witch.

You assume that times have changed, but people still preach hellfire. Every morning, on the bus, a Seventh Day Adventist who attended the local private school would tell us that we would go to hell if we carried on listening to Nirvana and watching *The Craft*. We were dabbling with the devil, she said.

One autumn, a coven came to our village. They wanted to practise rituals in the woods. These rituals, it was rumoured, involved the women dancing naked around a bonfire. Local chapels and their congregations were up in arms about it. This was in the nineties.

The first true 'crazy cat ladies' started appearing in newspapers in the nineteenth century. One of the first was New York's Rosalie 'Catty' Goodman, whose house was filled with cats after she was moved by the death of a kitten and decided to offer asylum to all the cats that had been turned out into the cold to starve. She had at least fifty, and despite complaints was allowed to keep them – unlike London's Countess de la Torre, who in 1887 was ordered to destroy her many cats after her neighbours protested. 'I have no other tie in the world but my cats,' she told a reporter, 'no one to care for, no one to care for me.' He is clearly sympathetic, saying that only the smell hints at her fondness for taking in poor, sick animals, and reporting how a number of her pets have been dying as a result of deliberate strychnine poisoning. 'Are we living in the Middle Ages?' she asks. 'Will they duck me? Or will the ordeal be by fire?'

I did not know that you could love a cat so much. I did not expect it.

I was aware of the women artists who adored their cats: of Suzanne Valadon, who fed her cats caviar and painted affectionate portraits of her ginger cat Raminou, along with several depictions of herself or other women holding their cats in their arms. And of Lois Mailou Jones, who painted with a kitten on her shoulder; Leonor Fini, who kept two dozen cats as pets and produced a book of cat lithographs. The cats ate and slept with her, and also summered with her, decamping in her car to the Loire Valley every August. Cat hairs even made their way on to her canvases after becoming fixed into the paint, which is no surprise, as by all accounts they climbed on her easel and palette while she worked. Also of Gertrude Abercrombie, the self-styled witch whose images of cats embodied a surrealist preoccupation with the unconscious, and left an impression of moonlight and sorcery.

I suppose in some way I thought these women eccentric, as artists often are. I didn't have the second sight, so I couldn't predict myself becoming so taken with my own cat that I would end up commissioning a portrait of her – from the poet Amy Key – a year down the line.

I had loved Molly, and Jessie, and Dudu, of course, but these were family cats: in the main part, my mother and father took care of them, fed them, took them to the vet when they were sick. As a child, your day-to-day interactions with a cat mostly involve pestering it, at least until the cat makes known its feelings about having its tail pulled. Children love their pets, of course, but they do not nurture them in the same way. There is a different dynamic. With Mackerel, we are all she has in the world. And, because our world has contracted this year to mostly encompass these four walls and a patch of garden, she is all we have in ours.

Because of the presence of their surrogate parents, domestic cats never grow up, and retain some kitten behaviours into adulthood (hence the kneading, and presenting her anus for inspection each morning). So you remain *in loco parentis* for the entirety of your relationship, and like many new parents, a lot of the time you haven't a clue what you are doing.

We resort to Google almost immediately, on the question of sleeping. I want her in the bedroom with us, but the bedroom is across the flat from her food, water and litter tray. Plus, my husband doesn't want to share his bed with a cat, and the internet seems to think that the kitten might jump up into the bed in the middle of the night. If she does this, we are warned, one of us could roll over in our sleep and squash her.

So we put her to bed in the kitchen, with a nice warm box and plenty of food and water, and a light left on so she doesn't get scared. I know that this is the best, safest thing for her, but the little mews she makes as she stares at me, wide-eyed, through the door's glass panels break my heart.

'She's a cat,' my husband says.

'She's a baby cat,' I reply.

Even now, when I think about the fact that we left her in a room alone overnight when she had just been taken from her mother, and how frightened and lonely she must have been, I feel intense guilt. I wonder if it has in any way affected her development, if this is why she is not really a lap cat, preferring instead to snooze near us, but at a distance, as she is doing behind me on the sofa right now, having finished her kneading.

But the internet was divided, and so I made a call. What else can you do?

How do I describe the kitten's personality? It is true that we chose her partly because she seemed sad. When we first bring her home, she is frightened, and, despite the fact that she needed to be protected, I worry that we have taken her from her mother too soon. This is the first of many worries, which seem designed to prepare me in some ways for the self-flagellations of motherhood. ('Perhaps I put you in nursery too young,' my mother has been known to say, when I express an anxiety about something or other.) Were we right to leave her overnight in a different room? Should we have slept with her those first few nights? Taken one of her siblings too? Has all of this shaped her personality in irrevocable ways?

'She's a cat,' my husband repeats, when I voice these concerns.

She is indeed a cat, but every time he says it, I hear the unspoken second half of the sentence: '. . . she isn't a baby.'

I know she is not a baby, because I am not insane. No longer insane. But it remains the case that she is a small creature for whom I am responsible, and I want to do right by her.

Despite my worries, she settles in quickly. She is curious, intrepid, lively. She loves our attention. When I am reading, she curls up on the pages, or tries to chew the corners of my book. She purrs with happiness, delights in chasing our feet and fingers. She makes us laugh with her little hops and pounces. She playfully attacks my husband, knowing not to use her claws, and in return he roughhouses her, pinning her gently to the ground and tickling her belly. Their favourite game is when he is using the dustpan and brush. She pounces on the brush, so he starts to brush her fur instead, until he has swept her into the dustpan and she is curled up in it, delighted. She's a cat, but she's also a new soul, an extra presence in our now atomised home, and that changes everything.

Camera roll:

BC (Before Cat), I took photos of friends and art and flowers. Then the friends and the art became forbidden and only flowers were left, so we added food. The shift in tone is plain: fifty photographs from the press view of the Andy Warhol exhibition that, it would turn out, would scarcely open (how grateful I came to be that I risked the empty train when things were already shutting down, the silent, grey banks of the river devoid of tourists, to stand for an hour inside The Exploding Plastic Inevitable, *the wild merging of light and sound lifting my heart like pills), then:*

My husband in his pyjamas, the bare earth of the garden, blossom, a loaf proving on the windowsill, spaghetti in kale pesto, ribolata, various successful attempts at French cookery. (Not pictured: the vile stew he cooked, which I described at the time as 'tedious', and which we ate for two days until we could eat no more, 'not even in a National Emergency, not even with Worcestershire sauce'.)

(Also not pictured: the row about the bottle of hand sanitiser that dissolved in the washing machine because my husband didn't empty the pockets of his trousers; my snide comments about his yogic delusions of grandeur; the strange, jarring feeling of being emotionally affected by a statement made by the Queen; the sudden tidal waves of fear and terror.)

Pictured: walks around the neighbourhood; rainbows in windows; graffiti – We Love You NHS/Unskilled Jobs are a Classist Myth Used by Rich People to Justify Poverty Wages; a beautiful asparagus quiche.

Then, the big weird walk into the city, the shuttered pubs and cafés, the tables on their sides like barricades (reminding me of the streets on the night of the Paris attacks), the barred gates to the British Museum and its courtyard, the invisible ghosts of emergency poncho-clad tour groups, the sadness of Trafalgar Square, the boarded-up theatres, the piles and piles of unread newspapers. It's Piccadilly Circus that is the worst, a ghastly place made even more so by apocalyptic advertising: STAY HOME, PROTECT THE NHS, SAVE LIVES/OUR LOCAL HEROES/FROM ALL OF US AT SAMSUNG – WE'LL GET THROUGH THIS TOGETHER, beneath which the only people around queue, mask-clad, for the pharmacy.

In a doorway: BETTER DAYS ARE COMING.

At first, lockdown felt like playing house. It was a shockingly beautiful spring, and the sunlight pouring through the windows bathed everything in a dreamlike tint. Time took on a hallucinatory feel. I collected posies from the garden and bought a check tablecloth. I practised my cooking, bought new bedding, threw open all the windows. It was, for us, a new domesticity. We had gone from being a couple who, while being married, lived unconventionally, perhaps even suspectly, with other people (I told myself it was bohemian rather than a question of circumstance – the sociopolitical aspect was too depressing to think about), to being a married couple who cohabited like other married couples. And in that environment, my desire for a baby – already at times fiercely, powerfully, irrationally strong – grew inside me.

I wouldn't call it domestic bliss. We were given daily death tolls, and the sirens – so many sirens – echoed through the birdsong, reminding me again of that night in Paris, and how it had felt as though the world was ending (for months afterwards, I heard French sirens in my sleep). It was hardly the time to think of having a child.

In a funny way, I was prepared: I have been locked down before. In the months following my return home after the Paris attacks, my anxiety became debilitating. Though it existed mostly in my head, the threat then was greater than any virus; it was all-encompassing. I believed that to leave my north London flat would mean inevitable death, usually at the hands of terrorists. I started avoiding public transport. I stopped going to bars and restaurants, because whenever I tried, I was unable to relax, always keeping one eye on the door as we had that night, wondering if they were coming for us, if they would kill us next. Every flight I took was destined to crash, just as every plane that flew overhead was about to fall from the sky.

I still went to work. I walked, or took a taxi. I opened and scanned the emails detailing what to do in an active shooter situation, where the safe rooms were, which exits to take. Whenever an alarm went off, I left the building and went home, where I would crawl into bed, hollowed out from the adrenaline.

It was during this time that my husband decided I needed a garden. There were three plots out the back; like Lisa's, ours was a bramble jungle. He hacked the brambles back and dug up every root. He laid gravel and made flowerbeds. I planted roses and lavender and honeysuckle, scattered meadow seed. It became a sanctuary, a place where I could be outside but still feel mostly safe.

That garden is the grandest gesture of love that I have ever received.

In the heat of the lockdown summer, I stand by the open window and watch Raj, our new downstairs neighbour, sitting cross-legged in a patch of evening sunlight, eating his dinner.

A deeply religious man who owns very little, Raj's first act when he moved in the previous summer had been to clear Lisa's overgrown, rubbish-strewn back garden, tending and tilling until it was a bare patch of earth. All spring and all summer, he gifts us vegetables that he has grown: courgettes and squash (as well as their flowers, which I stuff with ricotta and lemon and fry in batter), beetroots, chard.

I am moved by the generosity of this man. When the sickness hit, a 'hug box' appeared in the hallway containing masks, hand sanitiser and various tinned foodstuffs. This despite the fact that his work as an interpreter has ceased. The state is helping him with financial support. 'I am so grateful to your queen!' he says, one summer morning, as he commences work on the neglected communal front garden.

I am a strident republican, but I let it slide.

'I am praying for a child for you,' he tells me, the next time we speak, and I am vaguely affronted. What if I don't want a child? What if I had lost one, like several of my friends? What if I were infertile?

But it doesn't matter, I think. Let him pray. It makes no difference.

Another item for the gratitude list.

We both admitted, in a grudging, slightly shamefaced way, that we were on some level relieved that we were not going through lockdown in the same building as Lisa.

This was not tantamount to being glad that Lisa was dead. It was more the feeling that she would have found lockdown deeply distressing, and that distress would have hung in the air like aerosol particles, wreaking havoc, infecting all of us.

No wonder we didn't talk much about having a baby, my husband says, what with everything that was going on downstairs.

He means Lisa, but also the cat shit in the alleyway, the rubbish everywhere, the smoke coming up through the ceiling, the alcoholics, the having to phone the police when the shouting became banging.

I never thought about it, really. It was just a fact of city living, as immutable as pollution, or crime, or homelessness. Unsolvable. Or so we had been led to believe.

Over the course of the febrile summer, the kitten and I develop a routine. I have started to wake with the birdsong, and my first thought is always of her. It is so joyful to remember, on waking, that you have a kitten, and so no matter how awful the news is or how persistent my worries about my family, I feel happy. She is always there, waiting, near the glass panel of the door, mewing her little mouse call, stretching herself out in various yoga poses. I open the door, get down on my hands and knees, and say, 'Hello, sweetheart.' She greets me, purring, rubbing her face all over me. Then I feed her – from a packet, now that she is on solid food – again on my knees, so she can climb up and have a taste of today's menu straight from the packet – would mademoiselle prefer the minced salmon, or the tuna?

Three or four times a week, I leave to swim. Outdoor swimming facilities have been permitted to open, and I love these dawn walks through the empty streets towards the ponds, my husband at my side. The first few times, I worry about leaving Mackerel on her own, but I soon get used to it. She is safe indoors, I tell myself. Yet every time I come back, I expect calamity. I used to believe that bad things happened when you left the house, and sometimes I still feel that old conviction rising to the surface. I have to fight it.

Two agoraphobic women in the same building: one who survived and one who didn't. I am the one who got better. Why? Mainly through an accident of birth, education, access to treatment, a solid support network, love. So many privileges were festooned upon me, ensuring that I would live.

Before Lisa died, she disappeared. We knew little of her life, but it became increasingly clear that things had reached crisis point. Representatives from various agencies showed up on the doorstep, asking if we had seen her (we had not). Official-looking letters piled up in the hallway. Some of the furniture was removed from her house and taken to the dump, and we wondered if she was being evicted, or if the squalor had become too much. Lisa hated giving access to her flat, and we had asked the housing association to fix the hole in the ceiling, so we had a part to play in exacerbating her distress. We wondered if she was in hospital, or hiding from the law, but it turned out that she had been staying with her sister.

One day, she was back. I heard her thin, rasping voice calling out in the garden. 'Have you seen my cat? I'm trying to find my cat.' There had been no one to care for the cat in her absence, and she had told no one that she was going. He had probably left in search of food. *I'd have fed that bastard cat,* I thought.

Lisa was near tears.

'I'm sorry, I haven't,' I said. 'I hope you find him.'

It was the last conversation that we had.

A headline reads:

'EXCLUSIVE: Jerry Seinfeld's Cat Has A Baby Stroller And Enjoys Weed!'

And I think, *Imagine a female celebrity pushing a cat around in a pushchair. Imagine the things that they would say about her.*

I discover that I cannot smoke around the kitten. I have one joint out of the kitchen window as she sits by my feet, then find myself anxious that I have inadvertently poisoned her. This makes no sense: when I lived in Italy, I knew a cat that was high all the time. She used to nibble the marijuana plants that grew in the attic of the mansion in which my friend rented a room. She would lie on her back with her paws in the air, purring.

My friend's living situation was eccentric. The mansion, a baroque palace with cherubs on the ceiling, thirteen bathrooms, and a room that contained nothing but fur coats, was shared with many others. The old man who owned it was in his nineties and lived in the west wing. In the basement, there was a record producer. Several of the other rooms were occupied by sex workers; my friend shared the attic with the owner's son, whom we shall call Marco, our other friend from university, and the cat.

She loved this cat, and was understandably distraught when she returned home one day to find Marco clutching a bag in his hands and sobbing in Italian. My friend spoke the language well enough to just about discern that the bag contained the cat, and that its burial was imminent.

They moved to the garden, where a full funeral was conducted. Along with Marco's sister, they gave the cat a truly beautiful send-off. My friend wept piteously, for this cat had been a companion to her during a turbulent time – it is not easy to move abroad. They all said a few words about the cat. It was a perfect service. Italian Catholics know how to put on a funeral.

Afterwards, my friend went upstairs to see her other flatmate. This girl also occupied a room in the attic flat, and, being unable to afford the rent, had come to some sort of 'arrangement' with Marco that made us all uneasy. The room she was occupying had a large, circular bed, of the sort one associates with 1970s gangbangs. Being extraordinarily beautiful and therefore a veteran of male sleaze – she once attended a dinner hosted by Silvio Berlusconi – this didn't seem to alarm its occupant in the slightest. We called it the sex bed.

Anyway, when my grieving friend came upstairs, she was surprised to see the cat alive and well, curled up on the sex bed, minding its own business, and probably high.

This, naturally, raised questions about the memorial she had just attended.

It turned out the service had been for a small dog belonging to Marco's sister, upon which my friend had never laid eyes. Of course, in those days, our whole lives were one big linguistic mishap, but telling your Italian tutor that you had spent your weekend with your genitals (the Italian for parents is 'genitori') was a different matter to the offering of tearful eulogies to dogs you'd never met.

'Good lord,' I said, after I had stopped laughing. 'They must have thought you were very sensitive.'

When Tracey Emin's beloved cat, Docket, died in February 2020, she held a funeral for him that made the papers. 'I never knew I could love an animal so much, but it is a joining of souls,' she had said in the past. Docket had appeared in much of Tracey's work, and she has described him as her 'baby' and the thing that she loves most in the world. In 2012, she produced a book of photographs of him called *Because I Love Him*.

As in the case of Gwen John's cat, Tiger, Docket went missing in 2002, but was later found. The 'Lost Cat' posters Emin pasted around east London were valued at £500 and stolen by her neighbours. White Cube denied that they were art, though some art historians argued that the posters were a sort of trademark, working as Emin did according to several visual codes, and always autobiographically. To this day, the posters occasionally turn up on eBay. Docket came home, no thanks to the poster thieves.

People don't take cat-love seriously.

A month after the kitten comes to live with us, I celebrate my birthday. It is the sort of bright summer day that always makes me thankful that I was born in June. We lie on a mattress in the shade of a tree, and I read and sunbathe. A friend comes to see me (by June, we are permitted visitors in the garden). My in-laws send me a beautiful bunch of peonies.

Later on, after my friend has left, it starts to rain, and I say that we will have to eat indoors. But when there is a break in the weather, my husband is insistent. He goes down to the garden and puts a cloth on the table and lights candles. He cooks pasta rich with 'nduja, lemon and mascarpone, and we eat outside in the slightly cool, damp air at 9pm, just as the sky is beginning to darken. The garden smells of petrichor and garlic. *This is why I love him*, I think. I am thirty-three.

The next day, I am unable to get out of bed. The colour has drained from the world entirely. It strikes me that I would be better off dead. I lie there, noticing the feeling. *Hello, old friend*, I think. *It's been a while.* I feel, for the first time in my life, old.

Two months after the Paris attacks, when I was still reeling from the terror, we flew to Budapest. Thinking that I would die that night had reactivated all the emotions I had experienced the last time that I had thought I would die, to the point that I now thought I would die, or was in the process of dying, all the time.

In order to board the plane on which I thought I would die, I had necked two large glasses of white wine, along with two codeine, and this had resulted in me passing out and needing to be given oxygen by the cabin crew while I lay prone in the aisle. In some circles, such excess would see me labelled a 'legend' and my shenanigans would be perceived as an excellent start to the holiday, but I did not move in those circles. My circle consisted only of a tired and worried husband.

Really, I had no business travelling anywhere, believing as I did that there were gunmen around every corner who would almost certainly get me, if the terminal lung cancer, brain tumour, multiple sclerosis and liver disease from which I was convinced I was suffering didn't get me first. Because of this, the minibreak to Budapest was not entirely stress-free. The part I enjoyed most was the night we stayed in the hotel and ordered martinis to our room until I was too drunk to care if I was murdered in the middle of dinner, upon which point we went out vodka tasting.

The rest of the time, I was a neurotic nightmare. It is for this reason that, one day, we stopped at a souvenir stall and purchased Basil. Basil was a little cross-eyed cat, hand-carved from polished grey stone, no more than two inches thick. I decided that, as long as I had Basil on my person, nothing bad could happen to me. He became my talisman.

In Japan, beckoning cats, or *maneki-neko*, are considered lucky to the owners. In Tokyo, there is a whole Buddhist temple full of them, paws raised in unison. I have never been to Japan, but my husband was raised in a Buddhist household, while my father always used to tell Jehovah's Witnesses that he was Buddhist in order to get them to leave. 'I've never seen you meditate,' the nine-year-old me once pointed out. 'I'm meditating now,' my father retorted.

Basil was not a permanent solution to my issues, which required long-term therapeutic treatment and medication, but in a small way, he helped, by giving me the courage to venture outside. Whenever I was feeling particularly frightened, or could feel a panic attack coming on, I would reach into my pocket and stroke Basil. Trauma had turned me into a frightened child, and I needed a child's comforts to move through the world.

Then one day, when I no longer needed Basil, he disappeared. I do not generally lose things, and have occasionally searched for him, but to no avail. In a way, I'm glad he has gone. Magical thinking only gets you so far. There comes a point where you have to go it alone.

Perhaps it is because my own trauma is in remission that I decide to take on the traumas of others for a newspaper assignment, interviewing health workers and the psychologists treating them about the things that they have seen and heard during the pandemic's first wave. They will talk about the beeping from the machines following them home, the patients gasping for breath, the terrible moral injury of deciding who gets to live and who has to die. A story of how one care worker washed all the dead bodies of the residents before going home to cook dinner for her children will follow me around for weeks.

Why do I decide to do it? Partly, I think, because I know that I am lucky. To know that frightened animal feeling but to have survived. To be safe in this flat with my husband and my cat (who is perched on my desk, purring, as I write this). I do it because I know, after this year, there will be thousands more people who know that feeling, and not all of them will be able to live with it. Not all of them will survive it.

~

There are many ways in which a cat can die. The cat can disappear, like Smith and Molly and Lisa's bastard cat. They can be attacked by other animals: Watford, my mother's cat before I was born, was torn apart by a pit bull, while Jimi/ Tiger was savaged by a fox. Another of my mother's cats, Jones, went to sleep in a parking space, having possibly inhaled a few too many glue fumes during home improvements, only to be run over.

It is only when we get Mackerel that I become acutely aware of all the possible deaths that await her. Sometimes, a cat can have a good death. Jessie, born on my sixth birthday, died when I was twenty-six. Dudu had gone a couple of years before, also at a grand old age. He had tried to go behind the sofa, but eventually settled on curling up on the carpet, where we lay with him, weeping and caressing him, until his ragged breath stopped and he dribbled no more.

It is this sort of death that I would like for Mackerel, rather than to see her hit by a car, as Rosa – my dad's cat after Jessie – was, a death that tore him up. A disappearance isn't much better. I didn't want to have to select a photo for the posters that I would then have to put around the neighbourhood, competing for attention with all the other 'Lost Cat' posters. I didn't want to stand in the garden crying, as Lisa had, calling out for her in vain.

Fear is the price we pay for love, my mother says. But what if you have too much fear? What if the fear swallows up the love and becomes a prison for its object? I was well aware of my body's capacity for fear, how it could become flooded with it until it perceived the world only as a series of traps. I didn't want to be that kind of cat owner, just as I didn't want to be that kind of mother.

Perhaps I will never be a mother at all, I think, in the midst of my deep post-birthday depression. I lie for a week in my bed, contemplating death and the pointlessness of everything. Sadness is, I reflect, a reasonable reaction to a global pandemic that has changed the world immeasurably, taken an untold number of lives and livelihoods, destroyed the economy, and hoovered up yet another year of my potentially viable eggs. But at the same time, it is impossible for me to sink into depression without, at some level, feeling ridiculous, like a drama queen, or a woman in a Victorian novel who takes to her bed. There's a sort of dual consciousness to my depression: I feel like walking into traffic, while on some level, I wallow in the self-indulgence of it.

Up until this point, perversely, I have been doing very well. I had inadvertently become a stoic and anxiety had become my armour. But I was not prepared for sadness like this.

I lie there for days, in absolute despair. On the first day, Mackerel, who has thus far shown herself to be fairly stand-offish in temperament, comes and lies down next to me, kneading the wool of the blanket that covers me with her two front paws before curling up and going to sleep. She remains there for the duration of this low period, even when I cry so loudly that it wakes her up.

After a week, I get up and carry on.

I have read stories of depression in which people credit their cats with helping them to manage their mental health struggles. I have also read of – and know – women who, deprived of the ability to bear children for various reasons – such as health conditions, miscarriage, abortion, relationship status or living situation – have found that getting a cat helped their grief.

Occasionally, there are lurid tabloid headlines about women breastfeeding kittens, and when I read these stories I am saddened rather than amused. No one seems to ask what happened to the babies for whom the milk sprang.

No one ever seems to try to help these women. They are merely held up as figures of ridicule.

It's so sweet, I tell the internet. I haven't been well, and the cat hasn't left my side the entire time.

'She's waiting for you to die so she can eat you,' someone replies.

The crazy cat lady is a cautionary tale: should you not marry, should you not have children, should you choose to spend your life in solitude but for a cat or several, you will die alone and only be discovered once the cats have eaten your face, and the police will struggle to identify you.

I think again about the cat hoarders. So much female sadness and pain, channelled into these little creatures.

I didn't hear the noise that Lisa's brother made when the police broke down her door and he found her dead on the floor, where she had been for several days, and I am glad I didn't, because my husband said it was the worst sound he had ever heard. It was high summer, and all the windows had been thrown open, and so I had gone and stood in the windowless bathroom, knowing in my heart what was probably coming, what I had expected from the moment that he knocked on the door.

Later, after the police and the forensics team and her family, who had congregated outside the front of the building, had all left, I cried for Lisa and for her sad, lonely death and her bastard cat. I cried for the child she had once been, and all the unknown traumas that she had been subjected to, and the bitter unfairness of that. And I felt guilty, because, as someone who was also traumatised, I had chosen to keep my distance. I saw the aggression and the squalor of madness and addiction, and I felt afraid. Not that I could have helped her. Not that she would have wanted me to try. Who was I, really? What did I know?

The night Lisa probably died, we came home from a concert to find the front door of the house wide open, as was the door going down to the cellar. Though tipsy, I remember perceiving in the hallway a feeling of just-leftness, that sense of a presence having recently departed in a whirl of broiling chaos. Somehow, in my dark dreams that followed, this feeling turned into a certainty born from an old Irish superstition that, when a person dies, you must open a window to allow their soul to fly out. What I mean to say is that I woke believing that those doors had been open because Lisa's soul had been looking for an exit. First she had tried the cellar door, and then she had left by the front.

I know this can't be true. But a small, vestigial, witchy part of me still believes it.

I inherited my superstitious nature from my mother. Around the time that Dudu's health was failing, my maternal grandfather was dying. This meant that my mother was away from home a lot, and could not be with the cat in the way that she would have wished. After her father died, tied up in her grief was also a feeling of guilt. She had loved that cat, and had spent money that she didn't have on treatments for him, but she nevertheless felt that she hadn't entirely done right by him during his last months on the planet.

She was thinking about the cat while trying a meditation exercise she had read in a library book about grief. It involved lying on her back on the carpet. The same carpet, now that I think of it, where Dudu had died. She had been thinking about her father, but the guilt about the cat kept interrupting, so as she lay there, she decided to silently apologise to him. *I'm sorry*, she found herself thinking, *that I wasn't there for you.*

It was then that she felt a warm nudge against her face. It was the way a cat uses its cheekbone to butt you hello. It felt, she says, like forgiveness.

Sometimes, even now, when I stand by the window, looking out on to the gardens, I hope that I might see Lisa's cat. I don't know why. I never liked the cat, and a new cat has chosen our gardens as his territory. The new cat is like a negative of Lisa's cat: black with white patches, as opposed to white with black. The new cat doesn't shit in the alleyway or sit menacingly on top of the fence, and I feel nothing for this cat, positive or negative, because we are strangers.

I don't believe in reincarnation either, or that Lisa's cat turning up would somehow be an absolution of the guilt I feel, which, I believe, is essentially survivor's guilt. I was mad, too, so how come I got to live?

As for the cat, well, it's that I never really gave him a chance.

III

Summer, continued

Why you should have a baby:

You should have a baby because everyone else you know is having a baby. You should have a baby because you are in your late twenties/early thirties now, and that is what you do. You should have a baby because you are at a stage in life where, when someone tells you that they are pregnant, it is no longer most appropriate to say, 'Shit! What are you going to do?' and offer to come with them for the abortion. Instead, you squeal and then, when you get home, you cry.

You should have a baby because your ovaries will only last so long before they shrivel up and stop working, and because, contrary to everything you were told in your teens, one slip is not enough to render you immediately pregnant.

You should have a baby because you are a woman, and women have babies. Otherwise, what are you supposed to do? You have been told that you should have a baby because there is a whole dimension of human experience that you are missing out on. When people tell you this, you want to point out that there are infinite dimensions of human experience, and to experience them all would be impossible. You have never been in a tsunami, for example, or had a tapeworm.

You should have a baby because you are married and

there are only so many topics of conversation. You should have a baby because it's what humans are for, and if you don't have a baby and then you die, there will be no trace of you left (except for all the novels that you were able to write because you didn't have a baby).

You should have a baby because it is the most magical experience, and even though your mother had a difficult time of childrearing and sidelined many of her dreams in order to do it, she still gets misty-eyed when she talks about it, and says that it is the most wonderful thing that has ever happened to her.

You should have a baby because every now and again you see a woman with a baby and think, *Wouldn't it be lovely?*

You should have a baby because there are moments when you look at the man you love and imagine his features blended with yours and juxtaposed on to the little face of a small human for whom you would cheerfully kill, and you think that it must be some sort of trick that the potential for such happiness can exist.

You should have a baby because when the longing hits, you can think of little else.

You should have a baby because, admit it, you want to look after something.

You should have a baby because all the older women who you talk to about it tell you to stop agonising and just get on with it (but then one of those women died, leaving her children behind, which makes you think you shouldn't have a baby).

You should have a baby because your friends tell you that it's remarkably similar to being in lockdown, so now is as good a time as any.

You should have a baby because you don't want to end up a crazy cat lady.

You should have a baby because you want one more than you have ever wanted one before.

You should have a baby because you don't want to have not had a baby, to regret that for the rest of your life.

None of these reasons are about the child, about the sort of life that you could give a child. They are all about you.

But I know, I tell the voice, *I know that I could give her so much love, that I could offer her a stable home, and so many moments of comfort and safety and joy.* It is only because I have not allowed myself to imagine her too closely. We must find ways to protect ourselves.

She remains an intangible shadow presence, a mystery, waiting in the wings for her call, who could so easily slip into the bustling darkness behind the stage, so that I never see her face.

She is always, nevertheless, a girl.

It is true that I have always wanted to have a child, at least in an abstract sense. It is also true that a large part of me still believes that my life would be much easier without one. *Think of all the places you could go,* that person says. *The art you could make. Think, too, of all the sleep you'd get.*

There are two photos of my brother sleeping that I love. In the first, he is four or five, chubby-cheeked, with long, scruffy dark hair tousled around his ears, and his blankie tucked under his chin. He has shifted around in bed so that his head is no longer on the pillow but in front of it, turned towards Jessie, who is similarly curled up on the bed, and awake. My brother's hand is entwined in the fur behind the cat's head, just at that point where it meets the shoulders; the scruff of her neck. Her eyes are half-closed.

In the second photo, my brother is about eight. This time, he is in my mother's bed. His head is on the pillow and his hair is cut short. He is sandwiched between both cats – Dudu had joined the household by that point – curled up on the duvet.

In these photographs, my brother looks peaceful. There is no clue as to the whirlwind of chaos that follows him when he is awake. When he is awake, my brother, who is autistic, shows little interest in cats or people. And yet, he had a unique relationship with those cats. They were clearly very fond of him, and he them.

I can remember my brother learning to speak, before his words fell away. We would do animal noises. 'What noise does a mouse make? What noise does a sheep make?' and he could do them all.

'What noise does a pussy cat make?' we would ask him, and he would respond, in a high, sweet voice: 'Meow.'

It is only now that I am thinking about motherhood seriously myself that I begin to understand what it must have been like for my own mother, to be told that my brother would never speak, that he would never have a normal life. To me, my brother was always my brother. But a mother constructs a life for her child when that child is in the womb – I have seen it happen with my friends. To have that shattered, replaced by something else, something that doesn't mean you love your child any less – indeed, you might even say that you love him more – but something that, nonetheless, will be hard, and painful, and will make demands upon your body and mind that are so intense that, at times, you fear you will not survive: I did not understand what that meant, before. Now, my mother's strength feels all the more extraordinary. Now, I fear I do not have it within myself, should something similar happen to me.

Since my cousin and his family had the fever, all has not been well with one of their twin boys. The younger twin, my godson's brother, has been having seizures. His father and mother, also a good friend of mine, have had to rush him to hospital several times. Months later, he is thankfully recovering, but they have been in my thoughts throughout this pandemic. My friend also has a history of trauma, and the way she has survived a difficult labour and the challenging beginnings of motherhood has been inspiring to me. I want to know how she has learned to live with so much fear. What's her secret?

This family, I should add, also have a cat, Sasha. Sasha is a hermaphrodite cat, adopted by my friend at a time when she was devastated by miscarriage. Since the arrival of the twins, the cat has developed behavioural problems and started attacking the twins' father.

'Sasha hates him,' my friend says.

'Is it because he put the babies in you?' I ask.

'Maybe,' she says.

We are all walking on the Heath when she mentions her fears that Sasha is becoming depressed. 'You should talk to the vet,' I say. 'They can put her on antidepressants.'

It is at this exact moment that I realise I am a member of the metropolitan elite.

How does it feel to want a baby? The only way I can describe it is as a kind of longing. (As an editor, I struggle with the use of 'a kind of' to add a *literary-ness* to sentences, as in: 'I experienced a kind of horror.' It is pretentious. But as a writer, I recognise it adds an ambiguity that is sometimes necessary when it comes to describing feelings that are anything but categorical. What I feel is like longing, but it is not exactly longing.)

I shall try again:

How does it feel to want a baby? The only way that I can describe it is that it feels like longing, but a longing that is so fierce and potent that it could gobble me whole, like the cannibal witch that supposedly lived up the valley when I was growing up. It feels like *hiraeth*, a Welsh word that is untranslatable, but which means to feel longing for something – a place or a person or a time – that feels like home but may never have existed except within your imagination. *Hiraeth* is both homesickness and nostalgia, yet contained within the term is also the notion that that nostalgia or homesickness is thwarted, misplaced, somehow frustrated. What you are longing for is intangible. It is that meaning you grasp for which is just beyond words. It is, like the word that signifies it, untranslatable.

Better.

'Are you clucking?' a friend asked me, a year or so ago. I'd never heard those words used before to describe the feeling of wanting a baby. It sounded so benevolent.

I am not clucking. At times I am howling. My wanting a baby doesn't feel like a benevolent ruffling of feathers.

It feels desperate. It feels like the niggling of a hook, or a cat's claws digging themselves into my flesh, somewhere deep within me.

In other words, it fucking hurts.

And yet, until I was in my mid-to-late twenties, I felt no ache, nothing. What are these maternal feelings, I wondered, of which other women speak? They will come, these women say, with the knowing certainty of fairground fortune-tellers, a certain, smiling smugness as they grasp your palm. Best not to leave it too late.

Sometimes I envy the women who don't feel it at all, and dislike the fortune-tellers for being, in my case, largely right. *How much easier it would be to not feel this desire,* I think. In the past few years, it has only grown. And then I think of the women who feel the longing and choose not to give into it, how strong they are, how much I admire them.

What a fine trick patriarchy plays, to put us on opposing sides: the women who do, and the women who don't (while the woman who waited too long, the woman who changed her mind, whose longing is thwarted, is dangled like a ghost-train ghoul above the rest of us). Divide and conquer.

But these are the women I love and respect. They are not my enemies.

I read an article about anti-natalism – the belief that procreation is morally wrong – in which a woman from Population Matters says: 'We have so much opportunity these days to do important things and be pregnant with more than children. We can be pregnant with ideas and dreams and revolution.'

Can't I be pregnant with all those things? I wonder. Or does growing a baby in there crowd out all the dreaming?

While my friend potty-trains her toddlers, we are trying to get Mackerel to shit in the box. We were told that she was toilet-trained, but she is still a baby, and we live in a big flat for such a small kitten: the box is a bit of a walk from the living room, where she likes to play.

When it happens, defecation seems to take her by surprise. She squeaks like a mouse, giving you a few seconds' warning, and then: carnage. We have learned from bitter experience that trying to pick Mackerel up when she is doing her pre-shit squeak does absolutely nothing to prevent the process from unfolding. She is already set on the path she has chosen, and if you try to remove her, all that will happen is that you find yourself standing there frozen, and holding a shitting kitten, unsure of what your next move should be.

There was a point at the beginning of the pandemic when it hit me that the people I love could possibly die, and that knowledge was so frightening that I wasn't sure what to do with it. The effect of this was to make me crave the comforts of childhood, which is perhaps why I retrieved my froggy duvet from storage. Froggy duvet, as I call it, is a duvet cover that I had on my bed when I was about three or four, which is covered in cartoon frogs sitting on lily pads. When I first realised how bad 2020 was going to be, all I wanted to do was sit underneath it until everything was over and it was safe to come out again.

You can probably see where this is going. About two or three days after we brought Mackerel home, she was playing merrily among the folds of my froggy duvet when we heard the warning squeak. We sprang into action, but it was too late.

'I'm not sure I want children,' I used to say. 'I've already dealt with enough shit for a lifetime.'

I'm fairly relaxed when it comes to faeces. With my brother, you had to be. His toilet problems were just another part of living with him and loving him. When you look after someone more vulnerable, sometimes you have to wipe their backside or clear up their mess. It's just part of the job. You don't even really think of it as disgusting: it is simply a fact, a consequence of loving them.

So when the kitten shits spectacularly on the carpet or

on my froggy duvet, or treads pooey pawprints all over the kitchen, I am unflustered. My husband, meanwhile, responds with intense disgust. *What a baby,* I think privately, while I go to retrieve the mop. It is beyond me how he can get so stressed out by something as workaday as a bit of cat waste. It is beyond him how I could not really care that there is shit on the floor.

Serious writers don't generally write about poo. Literary novels fall into two groups: those that don't go into it at all, and those that go into it in great detail. The former group greatly outnumbers the latter, and I can understand why. Toilet habits are generally not enjoyable for readers (certainly, my enjoyment of James Joyce's love letters to Nora, without a doubt the filthiest words that I have ever read, was greatly marred by their scatological nature), and besides, many of our greatest works of literature were written in a time when poo was unmentionable, and the number of men writing novels greatly outnumbered the number of women writing novels, and it is generally women who have to deal with the poo of others, at least historically.

'History is women following behind with the bucket,' Alan Bennett has the female teacher complain in his play *The History Boys.* It's a line I think about a lot, having been schooled in the fundamentals of caring at a relatively young age. Being tasked with the labour of caring, of course, is part of the reason the history of women was little studied and understood. Women were, I imagine, often too tired to write it down, if they were taught to write at all. Or they were too dead, from childbirth.

When I tell my mother about our shit-reaction disparity – that he is so much more disgusted than I – she speculates that men have a much lower disgust threshold than women, perhaps for evolutionary reasons. This seems to let men – who until a generation ago scarcely deigned to change a nappy, let's remember – off the hook somewhat. And yet, he really seems to hate the shit.

'You get used to it,' I tell him. *Just you wait until I'm pregnant*, I think, cackling internally. *Then I won't be able to go near the litter tray at all.*

I'll never forget the time I went to visit my brother and his carer greeted us, pale-faced, at the station.

'There's been an incident,' he said.

My heart began to beat like a snare drum. Telling a catastrophist that 'there has been an incident' is up there with telling a colleague with anxiety that 'there is something we need to discuss' and then arranging a meeting to talk about it for a week hence. *What could it be?* I wonder. Did he have a seizure in the pool and nearly drown, again? Did he dislocate a carer's shoulder, again? Does he have some new, distressing symptom heralding an incurable illness?

It was none of these things.

'And then he pulled down his trousers and defecated,' the carer was in the process of saying. My brain caught up with the conversation and I surmised that my brother had been caught short in the car park of his local supermarket and had resorted to extreme measures, which had seen him break out of the car, sprint across the tarmac, and empty his bowels in the ornamental flowerbed near the automatic doors.

I became inwardly hysterical, partly from relief. I also knew that in order for me to maintain my stony façade, I must absolutely under no circumstances turn to look at my mother.

'We've spoken to the supermarket,' my brother's carer continued, in the same grave tone, 'and thankfully, they've agreed not to take it any further.'

The terrible therapist told me that it was inappropriate to laugh about the incident in the ornamental flowerbeds outside the supermarket. It is one of the many reasons why I thought he was a terrible therapist. *Have you not heard of gallows humour? Of humour as a coping mechanism?* I wanted to ask him. *Don't you see the payoff is in the final line, the fact that 'they've agreed not to take it any further'? What were they going to do, arrest a severely disabled young man? Put a grainy CCTV photo printout of him with his trousers around his ankles next to the till? Press charges?*

Doesn't everyone have a story involving faeces, or know

someone who does? Isn't it a bit patronising to exclude disabled people from this well-mined field of human comedy?

Don't you realise, I wanted to say . . . *don't you realise that you have to laugh, or else you'd cry?*

Having to deal with so much poo growing up is probably part of the reason that I have always found glamour intoxicating. Poo is why I moved to Paris at eighteen, broke up with my boyfriend, and embarked on the life of a single girl about town. It is why I saved months' worth of waitressing wages and then walked into Le Bon Marché and spent them on a Marc Jacobs blouse. It is why I insisted that we all go to drink champagne at the Hemingway Bar at the Paris Ritz even though it would cost us the price of five drinks in the dive bar we usually went to. It is why I took up smoking, which I practised while sitting on the windowsill in my tiny attic room, wearing a kimono. It is why one of the extravagant, frivolous things I missed in the year of the plague was the experience of drinking a martini in a hotel bar, in the late afternoon, while everyone else is still at work.

A rich girl I went to college with once told a friend of mine that she thought I was in awe of money. She was wrong. Though it is true we did not have very much money once we became a single-parent family – you could even say that we were poor, though I still feel shame when I write that word – I never really craved cash as much as I did glamour and beauty. I was thirteen or fourteen when my mother first helped me copy an outfit that I had seen in *Vogue*: a pale yellow silk slip, from Dior. Like her, I love design, and it never seemed fair to me that poor people shouldn't have beautiful things every now and again – especially poor women, who have historically spent so much of their lives dealing with other people's excrement.

Glamour is the antithesis of shit. We should all have a bank of glamorous experiences to which we can resort in less opulent times. It means that when you're sponging cat poo off your childhood duvet cover in the middle of a pandemic, you can, in your mind, return to the Hemingway Bar in July 2005, where you sat in a pale, lace-trimmed silk dress drinking champagne, thinking anything might be possible, even that you might one day marry the beautiful Frenchman sitting next to you.

(You will not marry him, you will walk in on him in bed with someone else, but that's another story.)

As well as my brother's toilet habits, my mother also had to deal with the cat's. 'Bloody cat!' she used to yell, usually because Dudu was tormenting our other cat, Jessie, who would follow her, complaining loudly, throughout the house.

'Bloody cat! Bloody cat! Bloody cat!' my brother would parrot, in an exact imitation of my mother's voice. This embarrassed her greatly when we were out in public or in company – it was unmistakably an impression of her – and I think my brother knew this, because he would laugh with delight while he was performing it, would sometimes be laughing so much that he could hardly get the words out. 'Bloody cat! Bloody cat! Bloody cat!'

There's a third photo of him with a cat, taken after he had gone into full-time care. In it, he is much older, handsome, wearing a rugby shirt. He is sitting on my father's bed and stroking his calico cat Rosa – poor Rosa, who would be hit in the road several weeks later – and he has an expression of gentle, tender calm on his face. I keep this photograph on my bedside table.

Google search terms, May–June 2020:

Kitten won't use litter tray
Kitten toilet training
Kitten won't bury poos
Kitten solid food
Kitten chirrup noise
Kitten squeaking
Kitten eyes changing colour
Kitten hyperactive
Kitten zoomies
Kitten diarrhoea

Kitten best toys
Kitten eating paper
Kitten chewing wires
Kitten-proofing house
Kitten sleep through the night
Kitten vaccination
Kitten microchip
Kitten kneading blanket
Kitten attacking husband's hands and feet
Kitten chewing books
Kitten avoids me when I'm on my period?
Kitten sleeps a lot

Though learning to look after a kitten involves a significant amount of worry, as well as the need to absorb a lot of new information, it is plain to me that it is worth it, because she makes me laugh every day. When she's in 'squirrel mode', she dashes through the house like a creature possessed, making demonic, strangled noises while she tries to climb the woodchip wallpaper. She does these star-jump pounces in mid-air that demonstrate the agility of a Russian gymnast, but with a facial expression of intense seriousness. She chases her own tail in circles, never seeming to realise the fact that it's attached to her body. She is small enough to fit in my hand, but in her head, she is a fearsome lioness. When on the attack, she does a funny sort of sideways hop in an attempt to make herself look bigger.

When she sleeps, she lies on her back, so her stripy white belly is fully exposed, toe beans pointed to the ceiling. When she purrs, her fur stands on end, brush-like, and her whole body hums. Having her is like having every cat video I've ever seen replaying in my own home. I am beside myself.

In the first few weeks, I keep losing the kitten. The flat is relatively large and cluttered, full of little hidey holes perfectly suited to a small mammal. 'Where's Mackerel?' I will say, with some alarm, when I have lost sight of her for a few minutes. My husband becomes sick of the question very quickly. He is a more laissez-faire friend to her. While I am tender and more anxious, he becomes a playmate to scrap with. She loves to hunt him, pouncing from behind the sofa as he tries to go about his business, making him laugh, and he is happy to let her explore, trusting in her robustness where I fret about her vulnerability.

Since we got the kitten, I have become alert to possible dangers: bits of string lying around, which the vet has said could slice her guts in two; glasses left on tables that she could push off, smash, and cut her paws on; toxic cloves of garlic left on chopping boards that she could nibble at. I locate these dangers with a facility that feels almost instinctive. All I have to do is keep this small thing alive. I have been working on a novel – no easy task when there's a kitten tap-dancing across the keyboard of your laptop – but I park it and dedicate my time almost wholly to Mackerel.

The first scare comes one spring afternoon, when I exit and re-enter the sunlit living room, only to find her gone. I call out to her in the two-syllable singsong she has already come to recognise ('*Mack-rel, Mack-rel*'), but this time she does not come. I rush frantically about the house, checking her usual hiding places. My heart is contracting, I am struggling to breathe. Where could she be? Each hiding place is empty, and the panic grows and grows. Hurrying back into the living room, my eye settles on the open first-floor window. And I know what has happened.

A writer's imagination, mixed with an anxiety disorder, is a heady cocktail indeed. 'You need to relax,' my husband says, when I am sent into a tailspin by her disappearance. When it comes to worst-case scenarios, I can always see them all playing out in vivid, harrowing detail. I don't just imagine a terminal illness, I imagine the diagnosis, the collapsing on the floor, the expression on my friends' faces, the long, slow decline.

By the time Mackerel emerges, sleepy-eyed, from her new lair beneath the record player, I have already pictured her broken little body on the patio below. When, almost faint with relief, I pick her up to hold her in my arms, I am sobbing wildly.

It has struck me that, if I do have children, I might become an anxious mother. The thought of this, naturally, makes me anxious.

Was I crying only from the fear of losing Mackerel? I don't think so, entirely. It is true that I have come to love this cat with a force that I did not predict, but I have also used her as a distraction from thinking about the people I love, most of whom, because of the pandemic, are too far away for me to reach.

When I was at my most unwell, my conviction that my family members, particularly my brother, would die dominated my thoughts to such an extent that it became debilitating. Yet this was not a totally irrational fear. My brother has epilepsy, and has had several frightening seizures, including one that would have seen him drown in a swimming pool had it not been for the quick reactions of his care worker.

This year, mortality has been a simmering, ever-present companion, which I have mostly kept at bay. Sometimes, the lid blows off the pot.

In *The Cat From Hué*, war reporter John Laurence writes of how adopting a Vietnamese cat called Méo gave him respite from the misery of the conflict that surrounded them.

'By providing food and shelter for the cat, I was affirming

a life, however small and insignificant, in the midst of the slaughter,' he writes. Laurence would return from the horrors of the field, and finding the cat waiting for him would feel like coming home. In a climate of unimaginable horror, the cat made him feel safe.

It has been six months since I last saw my brother, whose care home is in Wales. Of course, you don't stop loving someone because you cannot see them, but in the course of this awful year, the kitten has been something to love that was right there in front of me.

In this strange half-life I have been living – a life without social contact, or the ability to make future plans – she is a reminder that I am still breathing. That I still have love to give.

~

The year I lived in Paris, I experienced a freedom that I have not felt before or since. Freedom from caring, in more ways than one. I was, I suppose you could say, a bit of an alley cat: nocturnal, adventurous, of fickle affection, belonging to nobody. I would climb the nine flights of stairs to my little attic room in stockinged feet, having been informed that my doing so in high heels had led to the general assumption that I was a 'prostitute'. I don't remember this bothering me, particularly. The fact that I consorted with Americans only added further to my slutty image. Not to mention the man who parked outside my building for hours on Valentine's Day, drinking beer in his Citroën as he waited for me to come home from a date (I wasn't the first young woman who had been conditioned to mistake stalkerish behaviour for romantic displays of affection). Not to mention the other men I was seeing.

In those days, to become pregnant would mark the end of that freedom. We had spent the formative years of our adolescence being told how it could happen at the drop of a hat: it is ironic, one friend remarked to me, after her second miscarriage, that we spend so many years terrified that one forgotten pill or split condom would mean your life is ruined forever, only to reach the point where you desperately want a child and find that, contrary to all those scare stories, it isn't so easy at all.

'Why is it, do you think, that the kitten tends to avoid coming close to me when I'm on my period?' I ask my husband.

'Probably for many of the same reasons that I do,' he replies, smiling.

I choose to believe that he is joking.

It is true that the longing ebbs and flows, along with my cycle. Every month, just before my period, I become consumed with sadness and fury, mostly at the fact that I am not yet a mother. I want to tear my entire life down, set it all on fire and start again in some foreign place, alone. It's as though I feel the grief of losing my old life before I've even jettisoned it, and I become lachrymose and mournful and hideous to be around. The people around me have no words with which to comfort me, and within all their actions and gestures are hidden slights that only leave me feeling rejected.

At other, less hormonal times, I tell myself that I needn't become a mother at all. I am all logic. I watch footage of ambulances queued outside hospitals and forests burning and polar bears scavenging through bins for food, and I think, *It would be an act of madness to bring a child into this.*

(I was on my way home late one night when I watched the video of the polar bear, and when I got back, I sobbed beneath the duvet like my heart was breaking. It was a midnight deluge, as though the late hour had somehow opened the floodgates of an environmental grief that had been pooling within me. My poor husband. When he asked me what was wrong, I could scarcely get the words out. 'The bears,' I said. 'The bears.')

Better not, I reason. *Better not.*

I read an article about the BirthStrike movement, whose members vow 'not to bear children due to the severity of the ecological crisis'. Unlike anti-natalism, it doesn't declare it morally wrong to bring sentient beings into a world in which they will suffer. Nor does it subscribe to eugenic policies of population reduction. Its members simply want their radical act to raise awareness, and it also acts as a support group.

The founder, Blythe Pepino, tells the journalist that withdrawing her reproductive labour is 'in a sense, a very hopeful act. We're not just making this decision, hiding it and giving it up. We're politicising that decision – and hoping that will give us the chance to change our minds.'

We watch Holly and her boyfriend get married in a park in Brooklyn through a grainy laptop screen to a soundtrack of buskers' jazz, in a dress she ordered via next-day delivery. The ceremony is presided over by a guy from their street who just happened to be ordained, found using Facebook. The guests are scattered, forming a virtual mosaic: the bride's mother wears a fascinator and holds a champagne flute to the ceiling. The bridesmaids are all in London: I am on the sofa with my husband and my cat; R's tipsy face is squished next to E's, their features lit against the dark background of a bar smoking area; EM is with a new lover. He is handsome, and wearing only a towel, and she has that look on her face.

In a perfect New York moment, a drunk wanders into

the ceremony and has to be persuaded to retreat, and I cry more than I would were I sat in a pew or on a hay bale in a done-up barn. It has the romance of a war marriage, and we have all been made soft this strange, sad year.

It would be prosaic to state that nothing ever turns out as you had planned. This has been a year of disappointments: of cancelled trips and weddings, lost jobs, house purchases fallen through, of still-empty wombs. And yet it feels somehow right that the friend who lived in the airing cupboard, my partner in crime and comrade of similarly slender means, should be gifted this mad, beautiful wedding. This happiness. This love.

Everyone seems to have just had a baby or to be pregnant. We joke about contributing photos of Mackerel to the constant stream of baby pictures. Of countering the anecdotes of new parenthood with our own – 'Mackerel does that, too!' – just for the pure, silly, ridiculous amusement of it.

We need some sort of parenting manual, but for cats, I think, after yet another fruitless Google session spent reading the unsubstantiated opinions of various strangers who really seem to despise each other based on little more than the fact that they had the audacity to offer a different opinion on wet food versus dry. Before getting Mackerel, I had been unaware of the longstanding outdoor-versus-indoor cat wars and, though cognisant that I really had to stop drawing comparisons between cat ownership and parenthood lest all my friends with postnatal depression suffocate me with a muslin, it did slightly remind me of the judgemental pronouncements they were forced to listen to every day: tirades against mixed feeding or sleep training, resulting in hushed confessions of guilt at the 'lengths' they had been led to in order to survive, even when they were on the verge of insanity, even when their skin was grey from infection and their babies weren't feeding. Everyone seemed to have an opinion, and if you chose the wrong path – whether for cat or baby – you were quite simply a terrible person.

We receive the news that our nephew has been born, and are sent a photograph of him meeting his grandmother through the glass of a living room window. It is the sort of image that would not have made sense just a few months ago.

I worry the cat is developing an attachment disorder. Born and raised in varying degrees of lockdown, she meets very few other people, and, at least until she is 'done', will lead an indoor life. When we go out for our daily, government-mandated walks, we return to find her sprawled parallel to the threshold of the front door, waiting for us, like a dog. She follows me from room to room, though often when I try to stroke her she is standoffish, her expression one of distaste.

She is clearly only willing to give affection on her own terms. Once, and once only, she falls asleep across my husband's shoulders, like a little fur stole. She never repeats this gesture, but she is clearly fond of us: she always places herself nearby.

Despite the fact that she is evidently dependent on my attention, I find myself desperate to please her. She facilitates this by giving me just enough affection that I get high off it, then withdrawing. This reminds me of being single in my early twenties. I find myself wondering if the relationship dynamic between us recalls that which I was conditioned to expect from men – except worse, because with the cat, I have to tempt her into bed using milky treats.

Not long after losing Mackerel in the living room, we hear a huge crash and come running. Though we didn't see it, we discern from the mess that she has fallen from a bookcase, followed by a cascade of books and a heavy laptop, which may or may not have landed on her. The poor kitten has skedaddled, but when she emerges, limping, only to lie down quietly, chin resting on her paws, we fear she has seriously hurt herself.

I blame myself, of course. She had seemed so confident as she climbed from the armchair to the shelf, three feet up in the air, that I had let her. I was drinking a glass of wine at the time, and had already had a couple of cocktails. About this, too, I feel terrible. Furthermore, I have not done enough to kitten-proof the house. Why was a laptop balancing precariously on top of a pile of books? What kind of incompetent slattern lives like this?

My husband is worried, but not overly so. He helps me tipsily send a few videos of our limping kitten to the animal hospital, but after that he goes to bed. I insist on sleeping on the floor in the living room, checking my email every fifteen minutes to see if the triage vet has responded, until I fall into a fitful doze. When, approaching dawn, the purring kitten jumps down from the sofa to nuzzle my face, I am overwhelmed with relief.

The next day, the vet tells me that nothing is broken, but she is in pain and will need medication in her food three times a day. 'No long-term complications,' he reassures me. The vet is a six-foot-something Irish hunk who evidently uses the time not spent tending to his five cats or treating wounded pets working out. I want to cry into his brawny arms, but, owing to the possibility that either of us may be carrying a highly infectious, deadly disease, I restrain myself.

No long-term complications, he says. Except, I think, psychological. From that day onwards, Mackerel hardly climbs a thing. As for me, I become more uptight about her welfare.

Some of it is displaced fear, of course. Fear that something will happen to my brother before I see him again. Fear that my father's tobacco-scarred lungs will prove too weak should he contract the virus. Fear that my already struggling, unemployed mother's welfare payments will be cut, leaving her destitute. These eventualities are not controllable. But a small cat? I can be her protector. I can work to keep her safe.

Towards the end of the summer, my mother comes down to take care of Mackerel when we go away to Greece, and I hug her, despite the risks. I am uncertain about all of it: the flight, the being away from the cat, the danger to my mother from getting the train. I have spent the week leading up to the holiday in a state of high stress, and my mother is patient and kind, pouring me glasses of wine, cooking for us, helping me pack. The kitten takes to her immediately, and this helps. Other than the vet, she is the only person that Mackerel has met outside of our immediate family, and there has been some concern that lockdown may have made her strange. But my mother is so tender towards the kitten, and the kitten is gentle in return. Mackerel does not react so well to my friend Jacob, who drops by and stands at the bottom of the stairs in the hallway to chat. He and my mother are discussing the challenges of being unemployed when I bring out the kitten to meet Jacob, who in the gloomy hallway must look dark and looming. She high-tails it back up the stairs.

'Don't worry,' I say. 'She's a bit of a scaredy cat.'

When I find her in the bedroom, she is sitting on my suitcase.

In Greece, I meet cats wherever I go (and most of them have all their legs). Cats are legion here. Some have owners, but many do not, or they frequent a number of different establishments. In this sense, they are not so different to British cats. When we first brought Mackerel home and I was reading up extensively on the pros and cons of having an indoor or outdoor cat, I came across a fair bit of hysteria on message boards about Dreamies – a popular cat treat containing an addictive substance and being used as 'cat crack' to tempt cats away from their owners and 'steal' them. *Or maybe they just like the other household more,* I found myself thinking.

In Greece, people seem less hung up on demanding loyalty. They understand that a cat is a law unto herself.

'What's her name?' I ask the shopkeeper, of the beautiful grey-and-white tabby that I have just stepped over as she sleeps on the doormat.

'*Puttana,*' he replies. Whore.

The cat that adopts us for the duration of our stay is called Dalí, after Salvador. (Salvador Dalí loved cats, and took his pet ocelot Babou to restaurants.) Dalí is a cross-eyed Siamese cat who technically belongs to the sister of Vivi, the woman who rents us the apartment. In the baking afternoons, I sit under the jojoba tree to write. There is a view of olive groves and I have a cold beer and the only sound is the cacophony of crickets – it is hard to imagine a better writing situation. Dalí usually sleeps under my chair or beneath the table, and when he is not sleeping, he is in our apartment, cooling himself on the marble floors. Dalí doesn't smell particularly good; despite belonging to someone, he has the look and demeanour of a stray. In this sense, he reminds me of Dudu, the dribbling cat of my childhood. Though he made a home in our house, the feral wildness of the street cat always remained.

At my request, my mother sends me photos of Mackerel. I do not ask her to send photos of herself, though until recently we have been separated for many months. (How ungrateful children are. This woman birthed me and raised me and is now caring for my pet while I swim in the clear ocean.) I miss Mackerel, and for the first few days, I think of her often. But then I become distracted by other cats: I greet and stroke every cat I see. We hire a boat for the day – they'll give a boat to any pair of fools – and travel down the coast, swimming in silent coves where the sea is so still and clear you can see to the bottom. The feeling of the ocean on the surface of my skin after so long feels like being kissed all over by some goddess of fortune. *How lucky I am*, I think, *to be here, to know that the world is still turning.*

We dock at a taverna that has its own jetty, and order a large fish. Next to us, a heavily pregnant cat lies on her side, bloated and enormous.

'Be careful,' another diner says, 'there's a cat under your chair.'

'Oh, we know,' we say. We have been feeding her scraps of fish.

At the end of the holiday, we eat in a restaurant next to the sea. I am flushed with wine and good sleep, and I am happy. A black cat with no hind legs drags himself across the floor and flops down next to our chair.

'You're not going to cry, are you?' my husband says, but he is smiling.

I do not cry. I have made my peace with the bedraggled cats of Greece. At the table over from us, a young family are eating. The parents are both in their mid-twenties; the child is just walking. He will not leave the cat alone. The cat drags itself around our area of the restaurant, and the child follows.

'What noise does a pussycat make?' the young woman asks the child, smiling at me with that complicit look. Perhaps she thinks mine are at home. *No, no*, I think, *only a cat called Mackerel.*

'Meow, meow,' the child says.

Why you shouldn't have a baby:

You shouldn't have a baby because you have lost your mind twice and could do so again. You shouldn't have a baby because you are already too old. You shouldn't have a baby because it will stop you from writing. You shouldn't have a baby because you quite like your life as it is. You shouldn't have a baby because when you think about not having a baby, the next twenty years open up before you, brimming with possibility and adventure. You shouldn't have a baby because look at how many women you know, respect and love have chosen not to have a baby. You shouldn't have a baby because look at how happy and free you can be without one. You shouldn't have a baby because you know that you do not need a baby in order to have a meaningful life. You shouldn't have a baby because your life is already full of children that you adore and delight in.

You shouldn't have a baby because you find it hard enough just worrying about the cat. You shouldn't have a baby because it would mean more shit. You shouldn't have a baby because what if the baby gets ill, or is severely disabled, or dies? You shouldn't have a baby because, when your parents are gone, you have to look out for your brother. You shouldn't have a baby because you don't even own your own home, and your line of work is insecure. You shouldn't have a baby because *you can't do both.* You shouldn't have a baby because you are not sure whether you can give her the sort of life that she needs, and that you would want for her. You shouldn't have a baby because you will be a bad mother.

You shouldn't have a baby because not to have a baby is the biggest ethical contribution you can make to saving the world. You shouldn't have a baby because there are enough people on the planet. You shouldn't have a baby because by the time she is ten, a quarter of the world's insects will be gone, and by the time she is thirty, half the Earth's species will be extinct. You shouldn't have a baby because – haven't you noticed? – we are in the midst of an apocalypse. People are dying, institutions are crumbling, economies are collapsing, and all the while, the seas are rising, the planet is warming. You shouldn't have a baby because there will be more pandemics, and more wars. It will be no place for a child. You really shouldn't have a baby.

And yet. And yet.

IV

Autumn

When I was about twenty-eight and hoping for a marriage proposal, I cooked a recipe from a women's magazine for 'engagement chicken'. According to the mythology of this particular magazine, cooking engagement chicken for a man almost always results in a proposal of marriage. I don't remember much about the recipe, except that it involved lemons.

Though the witchy tendency in my family is strong, I am ordinarily a very rational person. I only tend to resort to magical thinking in times of great uncertainty, and my willingness to buy into this woo-woo recipe indicates that, at the time, I probably was not at my happiest. (In my early twenties, I only ever consulted my horoscope when I was in the midst of a doomed fling. As with tarot, I was rarely seeking guidance – I wanted reassurance.)

Furthermore, I once co-wrote an entire book about the ridiculous things women's magazines are always telling us to do. As ever, being a woman seems to involve a constant push and pull between compliance and resistance.

The chicken recipe is not so far removed from the love spells we acted out as little girls, always involving apple peel and rose petals and boys' names written on rolled-up strips torn from lined notebooks. Approaching the whirlwind of puberty seemed to make us crave some sort of control. Or perhaps it was our growing understanding about power and who held it. Maybe forcing them to want us could tip the odds in our favour.

The thing is, my now-husband, then-boyfriend, isn't even really that much of a fan of roast chicken. It's too greasy, and there is far too much deployment of the word 'carcass' involved for an ex – but still wary – vegetarian. The only roast chicken I ever remember him commenting on is that made by my grandmother, who steam-roasts it, resulting in the holy grail of roast chicken: crisp skin, but moist and tender flesh. He loves this chicken, but (to my knowledge) he has never been moved to propose to my grandmother.

For a long time, he was as unfazed about marriage as he was about roast chicken. And so the recipe was destined to be a failure from the start. Not that this stopped me from trying.

Children of divorce tend to go one of two ways when it comes to marriage: they either avoid it at all costs or desire it beyond all sense. I was in the latter camp. I wanted the big day, the speeches, the ivory dress that I had seen in *Vogue* as a teenager. That all felt important, and though I knew that, like so many things about being a woman (my hatred of my own body, for instance), it had been conditioned into me, that didn't seem to undermine my desire for it at all. I wanted a fairy tale, it is true, but more than all that, I wanted a marriage, and the stability that had, to an extent, been lost when my parents went their separate ways when I was twelve (a bad age). A few years after their separation, I would leave for Paris, and my brother would leave for a care home. Our unit had scattered.

I loved this man, and I wanted him to be my family.

Maybe I made him feel he was enough, that we could be a family without children. That he was all I needed. I never lied; I thought I wanted them, I said, but for several years I oscillated. I turned the decision over and over like a stone in my palm, trying to reconcile that desire for a baby with my fear of becoming a carer again, with my madness, with my desire to write. And as I went back and forth, trying to make sense of this mother of all questions, I never really made him a part of that process.

On the other hand, he avoided the subject.

'Go for it,' the geneticist said.

Holding hands, we walked out of the hospital for children

and for future hypothetical children who may or may not have genetic disabilities.

That was years ago, now.

The terrible therapist said, leave him. He will never give you what you want.

I had articulated a desire for marriage and a baby, and though I knew that the terrible therapist should not, ethically, have been giving me such peremptory advice, he had skilfully tapped into a fear of mine: the fear of being the woman who waits too long, and in doing so loses both the man and her chance at motherhood. Was he speaking as a professional, or as a man? What secret insight did he have into my husband's intentions?

(It didn't occur to me until many years later that perhaps there was something else entirely going on.)

This was three or four months after the Paris attacks, when, on a street empty of others, we had realised via a phone call from my mother that there were men shooting people in the area. We had left the restaurant in a haze of wine and happiness, having remarked casually that French people seemed much more glued to their phones than they had on our last visit a few years ago.

'*Faites-attention pour vous!*' the waitress called. An odd thing to say, but I hardly paused to reflect on what it might mean.

When my knees buckled from under me as we raced to find shelter, he held me up.

I left the therapist, instead.

An inconvenient truth:

The kitten thinks that I am her mother.

My uncle sent me a 'manual' for cat owners, called *Catwatching: The Essential Guide to Cat Behaviour*. It informs me that 'an adult domestic cat remains a kitten in its behaviour towards its pseudo-parental owner'.

We took her from her mother, and fed her milk.

When I lie in bed beneath the blanket, the baby cat comes to me and kneads the wool beneath her feet, purring. Colloquially, it's called 'puddling' or 'making biscuits', but the cat book calls it 'milk-treading'. When kittens feed from their mother, they use their paws to knead the milk from the nipple. This is the action that the domestic cat, suspended forever in quasi-infanthood, recreates. She's going through the motions of mother-love.

After several months, Mackerel also begins to lower her head to the blanket as she kneads, as though she is feeding from it. A couple of times, she has done this while sitting on my chest.

'This is becoming a tad bizarre,' my husband says, sitting next to me in bed as the cat mimes extracting milk from my nipples (I am, thankfully, wearing pyjamas at the time).

'Agreed,' I say, but I don't try to push her off.

There's a scene in the novel I am writing in which the protagonist goes to the Tracey Emin exhibition at White Cube and watches her video installation, *How It Feels*, in which a young Emin revisits the scene of the abortion that nearly killed her and talks to camera about her experience. The young woman in my novel is not based on myself – she is an artist who does not want children; I suppose I wanted to consider prospective motherhood from all angles – but all fiction is, to some extent, a transfiguration of lived experience, and this exhibition appears in my fiction because, in real life, it moved me enormously, and I have never forgotten it.

There's a point in the video where Emin is asked if she regrets not having had children, if she feels that she has missed out on a particular kind of love by not doing so, and she says:

'Well, you can love the whole fucking world, can't you?'

And there, in the darkness of the viewing room, I laughed, delighted.

I find that I keep breaking eggs recently. It is as though I have forgotten how to crack them into the bowl, a motion that, for most of my adult life, has been familiar, an automatic flick of the wrist. *Where has it come from, this new clumsiness?* I wonder, as I watch the yolk bleed into the white, ruining breakfast again. *Why must this metaphor be so heavy-handed?* I think, as I watch the stickiness spread across the counter where it fell, nowhere near the mixing bowl.

Where I grew up, it was common for a girl to have children very young, in her teens, even. I knew girls who sat their final exams with their bellies bumping up against the desks, their sleeves rolled up in the heat of the windowless halls where our futures were determined by how much we could remember and regurgitate. And I knew girls who had it seen to, whose older sisters or cousins took them across the border to a more anonymous city, where the doctor wouldn't know them, and would tell nobody.

On the wall outside the religious education classroom, there were ultrasound photographs of foetuses accompanied by anti-abortion captions dutifully written in the rounded handwriting of teenage girls. In the science block next door, the queue to get the morning-after pill from the school nurse snaked around the corner.

There were tales of botched abortions, of a foetus buried at the bottom of a cottage garden, consigned to the same ground from which, beneath the floorboards of the house, a poppet stuck with pins had been unearthed. It was put back.

(Poppet is my father's name for me, a name I have always found comforting. But, as with horror movie dolls, the subversion of childhood innocence into something potentially evil and threatening prompts an uncanny feeling. This girl framed the poppet as a ghost story: we were sitting around a campfire, avoiding the darkness at the edges of our vision, where the light from the flames did not reach.)

The poppet and the foetus are not related, except in the sense that both are crudely human-shaped and share a burial site. But it is the poppet that comes to mind when I think of that time, and the dawning realisation of the body horror that could come with being a woman. It is easier to imagine a small wooden doll, I suppose, than a thing made of flesh. And I knew enough about witches by then to know that they were just women who understood the ways of other women's bodies; who gave them tinctures and potions for cramps and aches and bleeds, and who could make a baby go away, if that was what you needed.

According to Pope Innocent VIII (1484), witches 'destroy the offspring of women . . . They hinder men from generating and women from conceiving.'

I do not like saying goodnight to the kitten. She sits on the other side of the door's glass panel and looks at me as though she is a convict who has been sent down for a long sentence. She mews like a mouse, putting her paw under the door in order to touch my finger.

'Can't we just try her again in our room?' I say to my husband, whining. But he is firm.

The separate sleeping arrangements are not for want of trying. I have done everything that the internet has told me to do, even streaming a recording of 'Relaxing Music for Cats', which consists of fifteen hours' worth of unremarkable, vaguely corporate-sounding piano muzak of the sort you imagine that they play at Dignitas to accompany the life slowly draining out of you, or which your phone adds as a soundtrack to an algorithmic photo compilation that it has created of meaningful breakfasts past. Because Mackerel has the music taste of a junior accountant, she loves it, and it succeeds in soothing her to sleep. But an hour later, she'll be awake, thrilled at the fact she is in our bedroom, purring and nuzzling our faces. It is absolutely adorable and completely infuriating. I am weak, and willing to tolerate it.

I have joined a cat-themed chat group with various members of my family: a handful of uncles and aunts, and some cousins, all dotted around the country, all in love with their cats. As a result, I have been party to various boasts, including: 'Edward and Matilda sleep through the night.' Edward and Matilda are almost exactly the same age as

Mackerel, and from what I can gather, they are slimmer, more active, better-trained kittens, who sleep through the night, eat normal amounts of food, have probably read *Ulysses*, and are fluent in French.

My brother has never slept through. Even now, he is still a night owl. His carers hear him on the monitor in the early hours, singing softly to himself.

We used to sing him to sleep. His favourite was a gospel version of the well-known poem 'On Children' by Kahlil Gibran:

> *Your children are not your children.*
> *They are the sons and daughters of Life's longing for*
>   *itself.*
> *They come through you but not from you,*
> *And though they are with you, yet they belong not to you.*

My brother, who has never used full sentences, would request this at bedtime, asking for 'Children'. Aside from this, we sang mostly old songs: 'Scarborough Fair', 'Early One Morning', 'Molly Malone', 'Green Grow the Rushes-O'. These were the songs my mother sang to me as a baby, and which I learned by heart and then sang to my brother.

On occasion, during those dark nights of the soul that

turn men desperate and unguarded, I have sung these songs to them, too.

My brother's sleep never lasted. My mother, in the next room, bore the brunt of this, but throughout our childhoods, he would sometimes come through to my bedroom, clutching his blanket, and get into bed with me. I was never annoyed when he did this; my brother is not physically affectionate. As a baby, he didn't like being held, and even as an adult, when you hug him he turns his face away (and oh, I am glad of this, because it's been over a year now since anyone has hugged him). I suppose in this sense he is a bit like a cat: not so much standoffish as what you might call un-needing. And so, as with a cat, whenever he curled up next to me and went to sleep, it felt as though he were bestowing the highest honour.

I had a pregnancy scare when I was just sixteen. The local doctor had already put the fear of god into me, telling me the contraceptive pill was not enough on its own to prevent conception. Perhaps she decided to scare me because of all the other girls who had passed through her office over the years, girls who saw their futures melt away before their eyes, and girls who'd always known that this is how it would be for them, as it had been for their mothers and grandmothers. All these girls had had to make a choice.

I imagine this doctor thought she was being responsible, was securing for me my future as it had already been laid out: exams, university, a career, children in my mid-twenties rather than my mid-teens. But the anxiety she created meant that when my period was late, I was petrified. I can't remember if I told my boyfriend.

In the car, I asked my father about the effectiveness of condoms. He is an intelligent man, and knew right away what I was getting at. 'Don't worry, Poppet. I'll look after the baby, and you can go to university.'

Had I turned out to be pregnant, this is not what would have happened. But it was what I needed to hear. He was saying, essentially, that my life wouldn't be over, just as it wasn't over for any of those other girls with whom I grew up, girls who are now women with three, four, five, six children, when I have none.

In the opening pages of Gloria Steinem's *My Life on the Road*:

THIS BOOK IS DEDICATED TO:
Dr John Sharpe of London, who in 1957, a decade before physicians in England could legally perform an abortion for any reason other than the health of the woman, took the considerable risk of referring for an abortion a twenty-two-year-old American on her way to India.

Knowing only that she had broken an engagement at home to seek an unknown fate, he said, 'You must promise me two things. First, you will not tell anyone my name. Second, you will do what you want to do with your life.'

Dear Dr Sharpe, I believe you, who knew the law was unjust, would not mind if I say this so long after your death:

I've done the best I could with my life.

This book is for you.

My life could have been very different. I could be spending this pandemic in a small cottage trying to care for my children, possibly alone. Not in a rented flat in north London trying to sleep-train a cat.

Do I feel grateful not to be living this alternative reality? If I am truly honest, I feel lucky not to be a mother in all this.

In 'How Did I Get Here?', a 1995 *New Yorker* essay by Nancy Franklin, she writes:

The worst year of my thirties was not the year after I turned thirty but the year after I turned thirty-one; until then, I had believed that once I touched thirty I'd get to turn around and do my twenties again, with a clean slate that this time I would mess up in the right ways. It was a shock to discover that the mistakes I hadn't made would now never be made but would exist as negative shapes, cast in a kind of lost-wax process.

I think a lot about these words, because this is how I feel about the children I haven't had. Those negative shapes.

The school had tried, in a way. But by the time it got around to giving us sex education, we were way beyond needing their rudimentary guidance. This fact was set in high relief when, during a class in which we were supposed to learn how to place a condom on a plastic penis, one girl ripped off the wrapper, placed the rubber between her teeth and proceeded to put it on the model using her mouth, all in one seamless movement. We were fifteen.

Their other strategy was a 'parenting' class. This involved looking after a flour baby, an idea imported from a young adult novel by Anne Fine, which involved drawing a face on a bag of flour, naming it, and taking it with you everywhere you went as though it were a 'real' baby. The project was meant to teach us about the responsibilities of parenting, but from the looks of all the first-year students who trudged through the halls covered from head to toe in white dust, all it had done was provide us with a new choice of projectile.

Hardly any of the babies survived the week. Baby guts were strewn all over campus. One lost its life being hurled from the top deck of the school bus; another was disembowelled halfway through history class, while her mother used the toilet. On the day the project came to an end, we were supposed to present the flour baby to class to show that we had completed the assignment. The school's only serious goth, a girl with multiple piercings who had carved 'Cradle of Filth' into her arm with a compass, baked hers into fairy cakes, which she shared out from a Tupperware container.

In the end, my period came. The last I heard, the school goth had a thriving cake business, and several children.

In the weeks leading up to the start of the pandemic, I had been worrying about contracting a virus; not Covid, but Zika, which was being widely reported at the time, and which could have a profoundly disabling impact on an unborn foetus. We had planned to go to Thailand, but to do so would mean delaying trying for the baby by several months due to the prevalence of the disease there. I was not fully resigned to this delay, nor had my husband and I really discussed it. The desire I felt to become a mother was urgent, but most of the time it fomented within me as a churning grief that I was unsure how to express in any way except anger. And so in the months leading up to the trip I had become wordless and distant.

By late January, the novel coronavirus was tearing through South East Asia. We cancelled the trip, but the knot of emotions that it had raised were difficult to untangle. We needed to get away, and so, in the middle of a storm, we took the train to Cornwall, and on the way I listened to *Blue*, because I was.

It's hard to choose a favourite song on Joni Mitchell's *Blue*, an album I discovered when I was a teenager, and which has come to mean more to me than almost any other. The first song from it I heard was 'The Last Time I Saw Richard', which I downloaded illegally using Napster for the pure and simple reason that it had the name Richard in the title, and I had just been dumped by a boy of the same name. I knew Joni was for sad girls and I was a sad girl, but instead of the simple break-up song that I was looking for, I was confronted with this intense, adult work of great emotional complexity. As with all of Joni Mitchell's music, the older I get, the more I discover within it echoes of feelings that I have experienced but been unable to pinpoint.

It was 'Little Green' that I listened to on the train to Cornwall that February. Joni's song about the daughter she gave up for adoption in 1965, though this was not made explicit until more than twenty years after *Blue*'s 1971 release. It's all there in the words, though, if you listen. 'Little Green' is a ballad to a child who is being let go by her mother, who tells her to 'be a gypsy dancer' and 'have a happy ending'.

But the line that breaks my heart is this: 'There'll be

icicles and birthday clothes and sometimes there'll be sorrow', I suppose because it speaks so perfectly of childhood, and sometimes it feels as though all I want, all I have wanted for years now, is to give someone a childhood. Icicles and birthday clothes.

One of my favourite memories of my mother involves icicles. It was Christmas. We had driven from the city to the snowy valley that we called home. When we arrived, the entire façade of the house was dripping in them; an heiress drenched in diamonds. It was so beautiful. We snapped them off, and used them to chill and stir our gin and tonics.

She always made me birthday clothes, too. Pretty floral dresses that were almost Victorian. I wore them with a petticoat and boots, and a little straw hat. When I came across colour photographs taken by Etheldreda Laing over a century ago, of her daughters in the garden, dressed in a similar fashion, I experienced an eerie pang of recognition.

These two snippets in some way sum up her mothering style: a wonderful sense of fun, coupled with tender, nurturing care. Not to mention style.

'I miss Mackerel!' my mother says, after their time together. 'She is my third child!'

I advise my mother to get a cat, once she is set up in a more permanent living situation. She has, I think, resigned herself to a retirement without a man by her side. She says that they all want a carer, not a partner.

My mother has never pressured me to have children. She is open about the joy that motherhood has brought her, but she is not a woman who has ever been categorical about life choices. Several of her 'London friends', as I think of them, have never had children, and this includes my godmother, Spike. And so from childhood, I spent time around these women, and learned that there was more than one way to live a good life.

At times, my desire for a child feels all-consuming. At others, motherhood holds little appeal. For most of my twenties, I was fairly ambivalent. Partly, this was the complacency of youth. But it was also because my future did not feel decided. I could very much envisage a life without children, and though I knew that choosing such a path would involve an inevitable loss, I never lost sight of what could be gained in the decision to remain child-free. I still haven't. There are compensations, and I am tempted by them.

Joni Mitchell also acquired a kitten during lockdown. 'I was lying in bed last night thinking about getting a cat, and this guy shows up at the gate around midnight, meowing,' she said, in an interview. The cat is called Puss 'n Boots. There's a photo of her holding him. She's wearing a red beret and the marmalade kitten is in the crook of her arm. Eyes closed, smiling, her face is bent towards the back of his head in a gentle nuzzle. It looks like love.

'Look at this face!' she says. 'He looks like my baby. The high cheekbones and everything.'

I find that I am talking too much about Mackerel. My friends enquire after her, but not because they want to hear a fifteen-minute spiel about the difficulties of getting her to sleep through the night. Unfortunately, because we are yo-yoing in and out of successive lockdowns, I don't really have much else going on in my life. Yet as I speak about her, I am mindful of the stereotype about women and cats, of the idea that to express too much love for a cat is somehow pathetic, or inappropriate. And so I temper it with self-effacing jokes, before changing the subject. Later, I rush home to make sure she is fed on time.

~

In Cornwall, we walked along windswept beaches as the wind stung our faces, drank cider and ate crab, watched the surfers from the shore. It was forecast to rain all week, but these showers were punctuated by sessions of glorious sunlight and blue sky. We sat on the harbour eating meat wrapped in pastry, watchful of the gulls that, from time to time, would try to divebomb us, and watched the tide come in and out. I felt like a desperate child, a mussel clinging to a rock as the waves engulf it. I was that kind of unhappy where everything felt symbolic. In the hotel, heavily pregnant women breakfasted with their partners. As we ate our crab sandwiches, a woman came in to show off her baby and her friend who owned the café held her high so she could see her and said, softly: 'Hello, hello, little one.'

There's a poem that I love by Fleur Adcock, called 'The Inner Harbour'. I have loved it since I was a teenager. It's about, I think, virginity loss, and pregnancy (or a desire for pregnancy), and fear. It has been swirling like a tidepool in my head for years now, and it did so again as I picked my way through a mire of seaweed at St Ives harbour, thinking of shrimps and sperm and false hope, of how the language of reproduction and that of the dark, fecund ocean feel so fittingly linked.

Shrimping-Net
Standing just under the boatshed
knee-deep in dappled water
sand-coloured legs and the sand itself
greenish in the lit ripples
watching the shrimps avoid her net
little flexible glass rockets
and the lifted mesh always empty
gauze and wire dripping sunlight

She is too tall to stand under
this house. It is a fantasy.

The seaside makes me think of my brother. He has always
loved the sea, and many of my happiest childhood memories are of being at the beach. These days, his care home
is by the shore, and in normal times we would walk along
the sand together until we reached the lighthouse. Part
of the ritual (autistic people like rituals) involves walking
up the steps and knocking on the door. When we do this,
my brother will say: 'Knock on the door – Mum's coming,'
I think because, whenever my mother visits him at the care
home, she will knock on his bedroom door.

Throughout this entire pandemic, during the long
stretches where he has not been allowed visitors, my brother
has asked: 'Mum's coming?' And the carer sitting next to
him, or I – on the other side of a screen – will say in
response, 'Yes, in lots of sleeps.' Sleeps are the only measure
of time that my brother knows. Ironic, considering he's
always done so little of it.

In Cornwall, we slept badly, and so everything I took in was
in a daze reminiscent of my trauma when it was at its worst.
During that time I felt dislocated from the world, as though
I were relating to it through thick, distorting layers of glass.
This was partly due to the sleep deprivation I experienced

from the nightmares, and partly from a symptom known as depersonalisation, a disjointed feeling of detachment and nothingness.

It is, I once wrote, 'A ghost-ship feeling of not being really there. A floating sensation of being outside yourself, like when you are a child and someone tells you about the universe, or you think really hard about how strange humans look, objectively: our noses, our slender, tapering fingers.'

Too tall for a house, too big for a house. We went sleepily to the art museum and looked at the paintings, then wandered into a darkened video installation screening room. The picture on the screen was of a woman wearing a white house, or else, a white house from which a woman's arms and legs protruded. It reminded me of *Femme Maison*, Louise Bourgeois' work about the claustrophobia and identity loss that comes with domesticity and motherhood, various interpretations of the image of a woman with a house where a head should be. Except in this work, *Rooms Designed for a Woman* by Emily Speed, the house has engulfed the woman completely.

As my husband and I watched the film, a school group entered. 'Let's hope there's nothing horrific in this,' the schoolteacher grinned, as he shepherded them in. But if he was fearful of some sort of *Interior Scroll*, period-blood-everywhere scenario, his fears were unfounded.

The video was rooted in the feminist avant-garde, so was fairly peculiar to the unversed, but there was nothing traumatic about it. The children loved it (children, as a rule, relish strangeness), but another teacher or parent-helper objected strongly to this 'weird' work, saying that it was 'unsuitable for children'.

I was fascinated by this woman's reaction to what amounted to merely a slightly eccentric, playful work celebrating absurdity and creativity. She shut down the children's enjoyment of it and instead sent the message that there was something odd and shameful about being eccentric or transgressive. Why? The work, or her inability to understand it, threatened her.

This is not how I would raise my child, I left the gallery thinking.

I had always wanted to be a parent who took their child to art galleries, as mine did me, despite the potential for embarrassment. As a toddler, I once had a screaming tantrum in the foyer of the Institute of Contemporary Art. The exhibition had been about Situationism, which one day would be the subject of my thesis, but back then I wasn't interested: I had just understood the concept of currency and was more focused on screaming GIVE ME ALL YOUR MONEY repeatedly, mortifying my parents. Not very Paris 1968.

My dad jokes that this demand set the tone for the ensuing decades.

After I moved out, my brother's tantrums – or meltdowns, as autistic people call them – became steadily worse and went on for longer, and were tied in with obsessional behaviour that eventually left him and my mother unable to leave the house.

I have rarely written or spoken about these particular challenges of caring for him, not because I am in denial about them or because it feels unseemly, but because, in truth, I hardly think of them. My memories of him are largely happy, and revolve around our closeness as siblings. And so I think not of all the disrupted nights, but of him getting into bed with me. Not of the chaos of the house, of not having autonomy over my space and possessions – which were often damaged or lost or destroyed – but of the home we had together.

Is this why it is so hard to make people understand that care work is labour? I feel the difficulty lies in the word 'care'. You are supposed to love the recipient of the care that you are giving, and because you feel that love, the work itself is 'natural', and therefore not worthy of remuneration and recognition. What do you want, a prize for being a mother? Well, yes, actually.

We are told to reproduce for the good of the economy; of

the disastrous impact of a 'baby shortage', but to speak of a society in which the decision to engage in the work of mothering is structurally supported is somehow frowned upon.

We are not supposed to acknowledge the hardest parts. We are supposed to meekly accept them as another facet of the duty that comes with love.

I too am guilty of participating in this collective delusion: of idealising caring. It's been years since I did it now, and so the most difficult, agonising parts of it have faded somewhat. At times, my love for my brother colours everything rose-pink. It is true that, once, he pulled me down the stairs by my hair. It is also true that, after the initial shock, I barely thought of that particular incident at all.

Perhaps it is because of these contradictions that I have always struggled to write about my brother. No matter how much I do it, it always feels like an emotional excavation. I cry every time, and afterwards, the sadness does not dissipate. It is not true that writing prompts catharsis; if anything, it can feel like you are submerging yourself in sorrow.

I wrote a poem about him once, when I was a student. I took it to a writing group. It probably wasn't a particularly good poem, and I can barely remember it now: it had something to do with how he used to love to listen to records, and missing him. But still, I read it, and that took courage.

There was an older boy there. A philosophy student, whose

poems were full of highfalutin references to drugs and modernism. When I was younger, I had been taught to believe such things suggested tortured genius, but these days I would identify them as self-conscious. 'This is a writers' group, not a therapy session,' he said, after I had read my poem.

The message I received that day was the message many women have received over the centuries, that you cannot make good art from the intricacies and complexities of caring. That to show work interrogating the subject or reflecting on your experience of it amounts to little more than an excretion. No creative process, no editorial judgement, no intellectual rigour has gone into the work. You merely excrete it from your feminine brain, just as you expel blood and milk from your feminine body.

It contains no philosophy, no sublime insight, no transcendental truths.

It is discharge; nothing more.

Taking care of the cat has, in some respects, allowed me to revisit a caring side of my personality that I have not engaged with for many years. *I am good at this,* I think. It is fulfilling.

But I am not sure I could be fulfilled if I did only this. I can totally see why you'd choose not to do it. Sometimes, the thought of playing with her bores me senseless.

After the art museum, we went to Barbara Hepworth's house. I took photographs of her studio, which was also her bedroom, and read about her children. (I have long kept a tally in my head of women artists, along the lines of 'had children/did not have children', as though this is supposed to reveal to me some great secret.) Hepworth had four children, including one set of triplets, and once said: 'A woman artist is not deprived by cooking and having children, nor by nursing children with measles (even in triplicate) – one is in fact nourished by this rich life, provided one always does some work each day; even a single half hour, so that the images grow in one's mind.'

The house was serene and beautiful, but it was the sculpture garden that we were there to see. On the way out, I was struck by the sight of a cat sleeping curled on a wide windowsill. The cat was black, and I was enchanted by it. Hepworth loved her cats, and there are several photos of her with them, so it was fitting that there should still be a cat at the museum to her work. I asked the volunteer for the cat's name and the woman said she didn't know, but I later found out, courtesy of the poet Ella Frears, who is local to the area and the writer of the sublime poem 'Fucking in Cornwall', that the cat's name is Misty.

I walked around the sculpture garden, contemplating and admiring the work. The recurring hole in her work, a motif of absence, reminded me of something, but I couldn't quite put my finger on what it was. I loved the art, but it wasn't at the forefront of my mind. Afterwards, I circled back round to look at the cat again.

I read that baby fever is when a woman feels such intense longing for a child that all practical or rational considerations go out the window. By the time we went to Cornwall, baby fever had engulfed me. But another fever was coming for us.

At the time, it was still somewhere else, outside the shot, but I know enough about storytelling to see that it was foreshadowed. As a catastrophist and recovered health anxiety sufferer, I felt I needed to be prepared. I stood in the chemist, avoiding eye contact with the condoms and the pregnancy tests, and wondered if I should buy two bottles of hand sanitiser, or four.

In the past, the black cat may have been interpreted as an omen, but I prefer to see her more as a sign. Of what, exactly, I'm still not sure.

For my hen party, Holly hired a tarot reader. She wasn't very good, though I didn't let on to her that I knew the meanings of the cards. I drew the Tower, which means catastrophe, followed by rebuilding. Perhaps knowing that I was the bride-to-be, the tarot reader waffled on about building solid foundations. The interpretation varies depending on the position of the cards, but the meaning of the Tower is fairly clear: in the Rider Waite pack, two people fall from the top of a burning, crumbling tower that has been struck by lightning. When I returned to the others, I laughed it off.

The tarot reader wasn't completely off the mark – and was less circumspect with my friend. 'What did she say?' we all asked, after the reading.

'She said . . .' My friend paused. 'She said . . . my boyfriend is kind of a muppet.'

It's October. Mackerel is getting bigger and longer, her fur sleeker, her tail less pointy. Her facial features have matured, too; her countenance is more elegant, with the nose becoming more streamlined. Her eyes no longer seem so huge, her face having filled out, and they are fully yellow now. The little white patch on her forehead is far less prominent.

She is more active, too. She is able to jump from the sofa to the armchair. She still has her 'zoomies' – the name used by cat people for the animals' brief periods of frenzied activity – but she is less clumsy as she sprints from one side of the house to the other, and her voice is deeper. She no longer squeaks like a mouse.

Soon, it will be time to think about having her neutered. *But she is still so small*, I think.

I didn't write a poem again until almost a decade later, when I skived a baby shower to go to a small dinner put on by a contemporary art museum in honour of a visiting American author whose work I admired. Outside, he gave me the rest of his cigarettes, because, he said, back in New York he would be on childcare duty. There was a picture on the packet of a baby smoking through a pacifier.

The poem was, in part, about smoking those cigarettes instead of attending the celebration, but it was also about feeling superstitious about baby showers in general. It recounted a conversation in which a woman had told me that in Islam, they don't do anything before the baby arrives, in case something goes wrong. It's a bit count-your-chickens, she said. I think that's how I would be, I said to her. I am a catastrophist.

Not without reason. One of the friends who came to my hen party was pregnant, but a month later she miscarried the night before her wedding. There was no time for a burial, so the foetus spent the day in the mother-of-the-bride's handbag.

The heavy-handed metaphor gods are at work again today: this time, I break three eggs, their yolks congealing in the frying pan as I cook breakfast for my husband.

(I have tried to feed these broken eggs to Mackerel, but she turns her nose up at them.)

Joni knew what living with a man was like, about the frying

pan being too wide when he is gone. But it is easier to fry eggs when you are the only one eating them. Because I keep breaking the eggs, I have become nervous when I crack them, and as a result, there is less confidence in my movements, meaning I break them even more often than I did before.

I read somewhere that a woman is already born with all the eggs she will ever have. During a lockdown conversation with an old university friend, he asks how I have been after a long period of not being in touch. 'I'm fine,' I reply, 'apart from my rapidly depleting eggs.' He replies that they are having a baby imminently.

The birth rate has plummeted during Covid. One survey found that sixty to eighty per cent of people under thirty-five living in five European countries – France, Germany, Italy, Spain and the UK – said they were postponing or abandoning the idea of having children, and only partly because of the pandemic. They are calling it a 'baby bust'.

You wouldn't know it from talking to everyone I know.

There is no year of the cat in the Chinese Zodiac, because, the legend goes, the cat slept through the meeting between the emperor and the animals, and arrived too late to be assigned to the calendar.

At least with a quiche, breaking eggs doesn't matter. In my first au pair job in Paris, one of my duties was to make quiche for the children from scratch. It was quiche Lorraine, and I became very good at making it first thing in the morning before picking the children up from school and bringing them home for a full three-course lunch. This seemed excessive to me: why couldn't the children have lunch at school, with their friends? But then a lot of what this particular mother required of me seemed excessive. I sensed that she wanted to maintain very tight control despite her absence from the children's day-to-day lives. The father was absent, too, but seemed uninterested in the nuances and practicalities of quiche. Instead, he seemed to spend most of his time accumulating parking tickets.

Shortcrust pastry, eggs, Gruyère, crème fraîche, milk, lardons. I could make it in my sleep.

The time has come to have Mackerel 'done'. I have wrestled with this decision, just as Doris Lessing did. 'I rang up three vets to ask if it was necessary for a cat's womb and tubes to be removed . . .' she writes. '. . . All three, with emphasis, insisted the best thing was to have the whole lot out.'

It feels, on some level, like mutilation: why would I take my perfectly healthy cat and have her uterus removed, when reproducing is what she is naturally designed to do? And I would love a litter of kittens, like we had when I was a child.

I do my research and talk to the brawny vet. He tells me

that if we don't do it, Mackerel will spend every moment of every day trying to get outside to get laid. 'People say they are not going to do it, and they are back here within days begging for their cat to have the op,' he says.

'Imagine if, every time you got horny, it was physically painful,' argues the person on the internet. I read that if she goes outside before she is spayed, she will immediately get knocked up, despite being barely out of childhood.

'I don't want my baby cat to get gangbanged by a load of lascivious toms,' I say to my husband, who says, as usual, that I am overthinking this.

In the end, the moral and practical arguments win out, and I book the appointment. It will be a simple, keyhole procedure, we are told, and she'll be home by the afternoon. And yet I am engaging in what my mother calls impending doom scenarios: something will go wrong. I know it.

It's just a touch of the old health anxiety. When I was at my most unwell, I was convinced that I was dying of a thousand different things, usually as a result of phantom symptoms that I had spent far too much time reading about. The pandemic meant that fearing for my health and the health of my loved ones no longer seemed so neurotic, but, aside from the psychosomatic cough I developed in the first two weeks of the outbreak, I have been coping well enough in the circumstances. I now think I channelled some of that fear into the kitten. Maybe if I could keep her alive, then everyone else would be OK, too.

Then again, it's not as though my own gynaecological track record has been a picnic, either. When I was twenty-five, I lay with my legs in stirrups as precancerous cells were burned off my cervix with a white-hot metal loop, while those pesky heavy-handed metaphor gods played 'Fix You' by Coldplay on the radio, and my mother waited on the verge of tears in the waiting room. (They really should explain better in the letter. It is true that they say, 'this is unlikely to be cancer', but, strangely enough, the final word in that sentence tends to be the one that stands out.)

I was not alone, though I felt it at the time. When you mention your own 'women's problems', others come to the fore: the scans, the biopsies, the cysts, the agonising pain, the being told you might never have children, the STDs, the miscarriages, the IVF, the post-partum infections. 'Women are born with pain inside them,' Fleabag is told. We are the walking wounded.

Since dropping Mackerel off first thing, I have been unable to concentrate all day. When the vet calls, I know immediately that it will not be good news, but there is no way that I could have predicted what he says next.

'Are you sure,' he asks, 'that she hasn't been spayed already?' I am imagining him standing there, up to his elbows in my cat's blood and guts as she lies immobile on the operating table.

I tell him that I am fairly sure: that she was born in lockdown, that she hadn't seen a vet until we took her. 'The thing is,' he says, 'we can't actually find her uterus. Do you think that you could double-check?'

I say yes and hang up. Then I become hysterical. The word 'hysteria' comes from the historical notion that women were made insane by their wandering wombs. In this case, it is the cat's womb that seems to have gone for a wander.

'I fear that this is some sort of awful omen for my own fertility,' I message a friend, who gently suggests that I have been indoors for too long.

In my mid-twenties, not long after I had the precancerous cells removed from my cervix, I attended a womb ritual in east London. It was ostensibly for work purposes – I was writing an article on how hippie lifestyle choices had become fashionable again – and I intended to retain the detached, wry persona of the rational, sceptical journalistic observer. This lasted until I got to the door of a normal-looking terraced house and smelled the incense, which immediately reminded me of my childhood home. Here I was, in a room full of women, all of whom were in one way or another on bad terms with their anatomy.

My own procedure had been moderately distressing, but

to an extent I had filed away its implications – an increased chance of future miscarriage or premature birth, needing closer medical monitoring for years to come, there always being a surge of anxiety when a smear test was due – in a folder marked 'Do not open'. In contrast, here were women, most of whom were five or ten years older than I, who were dealing with real shit – miscarriage, stillbirth, hysterectomies, cancer – and they had come to take part in this ritual in the hope of some sort of healing. I could not judge them.

We sat in a circle and performed the 'rite of the womb'. This amounted to a sort of guided meditation during which we repeated a mantra about the womb no longer being a site of pain but a place of solace and healing. I noticed some of the women's voices wobble when they said these words. At the end of the session, the shaman, who was called Chloe, recommended that we bury our menstrual blood in the back garden during a full moon as a way of 'cleansing' the pain and negative emotions that we had come to associate with our reproductive systems.

I knew immediately that I wouldn't do this, but I wondered how many of the other women would. Would they collect it in a jar and hide it somewhere until their partners or their husbands were sleeping, then tiptoe down the stairs in their nightdresses to plant their period next to the dahlias by the light of the full moon? Would they cry while they did it, and would it bring them peace?

I thought of a young girl burying a foetus at the bottom

of the garden. I thought of all the women, many in the hours of darkness, digging, planting, the merging of flesh and blood and earth. Ancient.

Reading something about fertility symbols, I come across a photograph of Mên-an-Tol, also known as the crick stone. A trio of standing stones located three miles northwest of Madron, Cornwall, the central stone is distinctive due to its large round hole. The stones are thought to date from the Neolithic or Early Bronze Age era. In Cornish, *mên-an-toll* means 'the stone of the hole' (D. M. Thomas called it 'the wind's vagina').

Barbara Hepworth, I think, when I see it. I must have seen a picture of these stones somewhere before. I'm excited. So much of writing feels like dowsing for links between disparate things, but here I have found one that somehow gives a shape to what I was feeling during that cold Cornwall February, and what I continue to feel now, many months later, my longing.

According to local myth, if a woman passes through the hole in the stone seven times during a full moon, she will soon become pregnant.

A few weeks later, I come across a reference to the Piero della Francesca fresco *Madonna del Parto*, in Heidi Julavits' diary *The Folded Clock*. In the diary, she recounts visiting the Tuscan village where the fresco is kept and being unexpectedly overcome when she sees it. Contemplation of the pregnant Madonna's face is believed to change the outcome of your own pregnancy, and the floor beneath it is littered with folded scraps of paper: prayers for children. Julavits has children, but at the time of her visit she was plagued by anxiety for their welfare. She felt, she writes, that 'it seemed not unwise to deliver to the Madonna a retroactive prayer containing the hope that she could someday give me what I now had'.

When the Madonna was due to be shipped to the Met in New York, the women in the village became fearful that without her, pregnancies would start to fail, and so to prevent her from leaving, they lay down in the street. 'It's the women who fret about luck and how to keep it safe,' she writes. 'It's the women who foresee doom and take extreme measures to battle its approach.'

In the temples in Vietnam, in the temples in Cambodia, in the temples in Sri Lanka, in the churches of Italy, in the churches of Paris, in the churches of Greece, I stood in the dimness and wished.

Artistic depictions of the Annunciation – the moment when Mary is informed by the angel Gabriel that she is with child – sometimes feature cats. In Jan de Beer's 1520 work, we see a seated white cat; in Lotto's slightly later version, a brown cat reacts in fear at the appearance of the angel Gabriel. In Federico Barocci's 1592–96 *Annunciation*, a small grey-and-white tabby is painted sleeping peacefully in the corner, its cheek resting on its paw.

Art historians say that – as in depictions of the holy family, such as the famous *Madonna of the Cat* – the cat is used to represent domesticity. But I think in these depictions of Mary, old traces of the mother-goddesses and her feline consorts remain, embedded as they are within the collective unconscious.

~

I read that Tracey Emin has been seriously ill. 'I had fucking cancer, and having half my body chopped out, including half my vagina, I can feel more than ever that love is allowed,' she said.

'I don't want children, I don't want all the things that you might subconsciously crave when you're young. I just want love. And as much love as I can possibly have. I want to be smothered in it, I want to be devoured by it. And I think that is OK.'

The vet finds the cat's womb eventually, but he has to slice her right open as he would a dog. It was, he says, a narrow, shrivelled little thing, though she might still have been able to carry a litter. It happens sometimes, he says. No long-term complications usually, but she will need extra care.

He tells me this as I stand in the doorway in a mask, my face red and blotchy from the cold, my coat wet from the rain. My heart is racing. On the walk over to the vet's surgery, it had struck me that, if something happened to my cat, I am not sure what I would do. Throughout the pandemic, and the months of isolation from friends and family, my brother, it has sometimes felt that she is the thing that stands between myself and madness. I have been so terribly good at not being insane this time, I would really like to maintain it. But it is getting to winter and the sun sets not long after lunch, and I am tired in my bones. The cat has become all there is.

I wonder how many weeping people the vet and his colleagues see in a day, especially at the moment.

'Hello, sweetheart,' I say, when I am allowed into the room, a cold slab at its centre that makes me shiver. She is wearing her ridiculous cone, and mewing in fear or in pain, I am not sure which. 'It's OK, it's OK.'

'What's wrong with her breathing?' I say. She sounds like Darth Vader; each inhalation crackled, heavy and somehow wet. I am told it is the tube they had to put in her throat, and that I must monitor it, as it could develop into an infection.

Outside, it's raining cats and dogs, but our trudge home is the opposite of the closing scene in *Breakfast at Tiffany's*, the cat now damp as well as hurt and frightened, me trying not to cry, yet embarrassed at how upset I am, my trench coat soaked through, and not in an elegant way. No heavenly chorus. They don't make them like they used to.

We have been told to keep her to one room so she can't climb, but when we get inside, we expect her to be groggy, and have neglected to close any of the doors. The second we unzip the case, she is like something from *The Exorcist*: a demon cat who can only move backwards and at top speed. She reverses all the way to the other side of the flat, then sits in a dark corner, her eyes big.

She must hate us for what we have done to her, I think.

The seizures started when my brother was in his early teens. By that time, he was spending weeknights at a residential school, but still coming home for weekends. I scour my memory for how many of his seizures I have witnessed, but I draw a blank. There is a succession of static images: him lying on the floor, the green jackets of the paramedics, the movement of my hand stroking his hair back from his face, but that is all. When I was eleven, I saw a girl have a seizure on the floor of the science lab, and her prone, jerking movements, the drool at the corners of her mouth, her dark curls, matted against the waxy paleness of her forehead, are what I see instead.

For as long as I can remember, epilepsy has been linked

in my mind with death. The first boy I kissed later died, in his teens, from a seizure. And I was named for Rhiannon, a university friend of my parents' who died during a seizure when she was still in her twenties. And so the thing I fear most in the world is somehow wrapped up in the very essence of who I am.

How do mothers do it? I find myself wondering, often. *How do they learn to live with the fear that their child might die?*

My mother says, 'Once you have a child, you are forever vulnerable.'

I could do without that, possibly.

A young woman who used to babysit for my brother asked me once if looking after disabled people might be a future career in which I'd be interested. I told her a categorical, blunt no.

At times it has felt like care work is my destiny, and that, ever since I left home, my desire to write has been a way of resisting that. There's no one so solitary as a writer, after all.

My desire to spend the night with the cat is granted, but only through necessity. In the hours that follow her return from the vet, she insists on trying to remove her cone, and succeeds twice when we are not watching her. She immediately begins to lick her wounds, her rough tongue seconds away from rupturing her stitches. Holly tells me that her father's cat disembowelled herself this way, and almost died, and so I decide to stay with her.

I make a bed up on the kitchen floor. For the first few hours, Mackerel tries to remove her cone by dragging it along the floor and bashing her head repeatedly against the furniture. I will drift off at intervals, only to wake to the sound of plastic hitting linoleum, her laboured breathing, her mews pleading for freedom. All of this takes place to a soundtrack of 'Relaxing Music for Cats' played through my phone.

At some point during the night, I start to cry. The whole scene is just so pitiable, and I am unbearably tired. I think of my brother, hundreds of miles away, probably still awake, his voice echoing through the monitor as he sings to himself, because we are not there. Does he ever ask for his lullaby, still?

Eventually, we both sleep, though the floor is hard and my back is aching and the kitchen is freezing. When I wake, hours later, 'Relaxing Music for Cats' is still playing, though it appears to have entered a new movement. Mackerel is curled up next to me, sleeping encircled in my arms. Dawn is breaking. We have made it through.

Lessing's description of bringing her cat home after her spay resonates. 'She had been betrayed and she knew it,'

Lessing writes. 'She had been sold out by a friend . . . a terrible thing had been done to her. I couldn't bear to look at her eyes.

'It was not that she was very ill, or in danger. She was in a bad state of shock. I do not think any creature can "get over" an experience like this.'

I read this before I took Mackerel to the vet, and I still did it.

~

After she recovers, the kitten becomes less needy. She doesn't want to be stroked, and starts putting herself to bed. If you happen to still be in the living room or kitchen at bedtime, she makes it plain that she wants you out.

When restrictions are loosened and my friend Sarah – whom I refer to as my 'antibody pal' because she caught Covid early on and still carries immunity – comes over, and we stay up late into the night, smoking and talking, Mackerel morphs into a passive-aggressive flatmate, crawling under the rug and sitting there like a Persian-patterned lump directly in our line of sight, as if to say: 'Don't mind me, guys. It's not like I'm trying to sleep or anything.'

Sometimes, when I want to read late, or when my shoulder is especially frozen from sitting for too long at my writing desk, or when my husband and I have argued, I sleep in the spare room. When I do this, I let the kitten come in with me. She just needs to get used to it, I tell myself, and she will sleep through the night. But though she will spend periods curled up on the bed next to me, first purring, then dreaming – if cats do dream, and I believe they must – I always wake in the small hours to find her face up in mine as her body vibrates noisily in anticipation of a more engaged closeness: a scratch, or a stroke.

I never begrudge her, just as I never begrudged my brother for his late-night forays into my bed when he was small, and just as my husband never begrudged me whenever I had a nightmare so terrible it left me hyperventilating, haunted by images worse than any horror film, or because I heard the sirens in my sleep. The need we feel in the dead of night is primitive. It is when we cry out for our mothers, both before and after they are gone.

But then, I have never been faced with the endless nightcries of a howling infant. My mother hardly slept for seven years; I still don't know how she kept her sanity.

Before I left him, the terrible therapist told me that a child needs a protective boundary between herself and her fears, and that it is the parent's role to provide that. They must go into the room and say, 'There are no monsters here. I will keep you safe.' Anxiety arises when, for whatever reason, such reassurance is absent. He speculated that, because of the disruption and exhaustion caused by my brother, I felt, perhaps subconsciously, that I couldn't trouble my mother when I needed her to tell me I was safe. It is a neat theory, though it doesn't chime with my memories of how I would get into bed with her, terrified, after reading some ghost story or another (after reading *The Turn of the Screw*, I followed her around the house for days). My mother has always soothed my maddest fears.

I cherish these nights with the cat, when it is just the two of us, but I always wake missing my husband, and when he wakes, he always calls out to me through the door. I will go to him, the night apart, each of us in too-big beds, having cemented us somehow, even when we have argued.

After that, I'll go through to the kitchen and put the coffee on. For breakfast, we'll have eggs.

V

Winter

When my husband eats an orange, he peels it carefully, then consumes it with measured slowness. He always offers me at least two segments, usually three, and this small act of generosity moves me. I do not have the patience for peeling oranges; I always rush, jamming in my fingernail too harshly so that it breaks through the pith and the fruit becomes a sodden mess in my hand. And I do not like the sticky fingers.

But a segment or three is perfect. 'My mother always used to share her orange with us,' he tells me (his mother has birthed and cared for nine children, so I imagine being the chosen one to share with her on a given day may have imparted an extra thrill). And so he shares his orange with me, and one day, I hope, will share it with our child. I will happily forgo the privilege of sharing with him to witness that. I like the thought of it. Perhaps the child will go on to share her orange with her own child, or perhaps she will keep it, joyfully, all to herself. Whatever makes her happy.

A memory from childhood: standing at the mirror and pushing out my belly, marvelling at its convex shape, imagining what it would be like, this state, what I thought of as my destiny.

When the virus came, media told us of the importance of vitamin C. And so we bought lots of oranges. One of the first photographs I took and shared from our newly confined existence was of two oranges sitting on a little flower-shaped plate, cast in bright sunlight. 'I'm going to be taking a lot of still lives from now on,' I wrote, not knowing then quite how stilled our lives would become.

The cat recovers slowly from her operation. The cone comes off. The angry open wound heals. The bald patch on her belly begins to grow back. She has regained some of her sprightliness, and is pouncing once more from the sofa to the armchair to the coffee table. She has also gained weight: the small pouch of flabby skin between her back legs is sagging more prominently (it is known as, I discover, the primordial pouch, a phrase I can't help but find amusing: 'I'm not fat, it's just my primordial pouch!'). Throughout this entire ordeal, she has never lost her appetite. If anything, it has become even more fierce. I indulged it. It is hard to see an animal in pain.

The unexpected complications from her disappearing uterus have affected me more strongly than I had ever thought they would (not that having a kitten with a wandering womb was a problem I had ever anticipated having). The sleepless nights and the constant vigilance that was required to stop her tearing herself open no doubt contributed to the stress, but still: she is just a cat, after all.

And it's true that she is a cat. But there is something about looking after her that has prodded the carer in me awake. I realise that I have been using that old familiar role to sustain myself through these past months. Too much introspection can be dangerous, especially in times of isolation. This animal is an external force to which I could devote myself, instead of becoming overwhelmed by my fear at potentially losing the people I love. The kitten is a vessel into which I can pour all that terrified love, all those things I cannot say aloud.

Happily, my anxiety about her coming to harm lessens as she grows. Frankly, she's grown too fat to sit on accidentally now, and I am less worried about putting her through the wash. (I was told a horror story about a kitten that died this way, having fallen asleep on a pile of laundry in the washing machine, and as a result, each time I put clothes in the drum, I checked religiously, almost compulsively, to ascertain that she was elsewhere.)

Has she forgiven me? How long does a cat bear a grudge?

It is hard to know. After the initial post-vet love bombing, she is less affectionate, and more wary. Although she still comes to me when I sit or lie in bed reading, she is now happier spending time in other rooms, alone. She has found a favoured spot on top of the wardrobe in the spare room, and it is here that she spends her evenings, in the dark, like a teenage goth. Sometimes I go to her and stand in the gloom on tiptoes, reaching my hand up high above my head until my fingers make contact with her fur as she lifts her head regally for a stroke. She has the imperiousness of a deity being given an offering; as P. G. Wodehouse wrote, 'Cats, as a class, have never completely got over the snootiness caused by the fact that in ancient Egypt they were worshipped as gods.'

Really, he should have said goddesses.

Shortly before the cat's operation, I had walked into the city to meet three university friends. One had given birth last winter, and this would be the first time that I would meet her daughter. Another brought her toddler, a smiley little boy. The third came with the puppy she'd adopted during lockdown. I joked that I was sad to have to leave the cat at home.

We entered the chaos of the Princess Diana Memorial Playground for mere minutes before retreating somewhere quieter. My friend's son ran right to the edge of the duck pond and she hurried after him, our conversation cut short. My friend's daughter looked exactly as I would have predicted: like her mother, notably and heart-soaringly beautiful. 'Hello,' I said to her, 'it's so good to meet you.'

The puppy was a puppy: not a kitten, but sweet.

It was one of those crisp, bright days in late autumn: a first taste of winter. As we walked and chatted, I felt profoundly grateful for the friendship of these women, with whom I spent a year in Italy sitting in squares, drinking bitter red aperitivi and bright orange fizz and smoking long, slim eastern European cigarettes. We danced with abandon and cried with laughter.

A decade later, we have been there through the twists and turns of one another's lives in ways that I could never have predicted, and which still feels somehow miraculous, as does the fact that two of us are now mothers.

My friend with the baby girl is something of an inspiration to me. She has long suffered from an anxiety so intense that at times it has been debilitating. Sometimes the bouts of depersonalisation go on for weeks. Having only suffered that detachment from the self in short episodes, I cannot imagine anything so terrifying. And yet, she has become a mother, and a good, loving one. It makes me happy, and it gives me hope.

The night I was attacked, I had been with this woman, though we were not women then, or at least we did not yet feel like women. I had just recently returned from Italy, where we had become closer as we navigated the sometimes challenging experience of living abroad. You could say that perhaps it was an unlikely friendship, insomuch as she had grown up in very different circumstances to mine: a multi-floored townhouse not far from the palace, a school attended by princesses. But in the fundamentals, we are not so different: we love design, and dancing, and travel, and Italian literature, and have loving families.

We had been to a party in an enormous apartment that had been stripped of furniture; the hostess's parents were moving. I remember little of the party itself. I suspect my memory of it was obliterated by what happened later that night: lying on the pavement, a man's hands around my neck, his fingers somehow also digging into the flesh of my thighs.

After the party, I took two buses from the wealthy part of the city to a poor part of the city, ignoring my friend's pleas to stay with her; a fateful decision, but no longer one for which I blame myself. And yet that simple twist of fate created, in the theoretical physics of my traumatised mind, a whole parallel universe built on the premise of having gone with her. Somewhere, there is another girl. She never went home alone that night. Instead, she walked up the steps of a grand house that used to be an embassy and walked through a marble hallway into a lift. She went up several floors to her friend's bedroom and kicked off her heels, not in order to run down a dark street screaming, but to get into a warm, safe bed.

The nights are drawing in, and we are dreading the darkness without the usual compensations of the season: toasting next to warm fires with friends; red wine; the theatre; packed pubs with steamed-up windows; and seriously rich, unhealthy meals involving baked cheese or slow-cooked meat shared with family.

All such comforts look to be off the table, so we must find other things to keep us buoyed. As the temperature drops, I stop swimming outdoors on the Heath, but my husband continues, craving that cold-water high. On Bonfire Night, we sit by the firepit in the garden drinking ginger wine, wrapped in blankets, hot-water bottles resting on our knees, our neighbours treating us to an intimate fireworks display.

We take brisk, autumnal walks followed by kiosk hot chocolate. I cook boeuf bourguignon with dauphinoise, lamb stew, duck in a plum and ginger sauce, while listening to Billie sing 'Autumn in New York'. The gourds and pump-kins pile up in the fruit bowl, threatening to topple over, and we carve faces into some of them to mark Halloween, a festival my mother always embraced with witchy joy when we were children. I buy packs of copper wire twinkle lights and thread them into empty whiskey bottles, which I dot around the house, and as soon as the sky begins to darken, I switch them all on. 'We just need to shift the atmosphere,' I say, at the end of another working day spent trying to avoid the headlines. 'To make things more festive.'

But it is a challenge, it is tiring, and on some days my little lanterns look like pathetic, twee attempts at levity in the darkest days we've ever known. There is no cure, no end in sight.

The most powerful man in the world is standing for re-election, and I am sitting in on a virtual coven who are trying to prevent him from winning. When he was first elected, the witches became very active, and cast a 'mass spell' against him. Four years on, they are even more prepared.

I tell myself that it is for research for a book about the relationship between women and cats, which has a section on witchcraft – the book that this book was originally going to be, before all these questions and recollections began to intrude. But I am also here because, after many months with a man, I want to be with other women, women who also feel powerless and scared.

I took the last election badly. Whether a man grabs you between the legs or by the throat, he is the same kind of man.

It has been many years since I have done a 'spell', not since school, when we used to mess around inventing love spells about boys we liked (it strikes me that those incantations, too, were about limiting the power of men).

My mother, who I have told about my research, is concerned. It's not that she believes in magic, but since she abandoned the tarot, she is of the 'don't mess with shit you don't understand' school of superstition. She implores me to draw an invisible circle around myself. I tell her that I will, though I stress that the coven are not performing 'dark magic': the spell is a binding spell, to prevent the man and his henchmen from doing harm to others.

The lead witch has a cat that she calls her familiar. I sit with my camera off, having assembled all the required components, which are as follows:

- Tower tarot card (from any deck)
- Tiny stub of an orange candle
- Pin or small nail (to inscribe candle)
- White candle (any size), representing the element of Fire
- Small bowl of water, representing elemental Water
- Small bowl of salt, representing elemental Earth
- Feather (any), representing the element of Air
- Matches or lighter
- Ashtray or dish of sand

Optional:

- Piece of pyrite (fool's gold)
- Sulphur
- Black thread (for traditional binding variant)
- Baby carrot (as substitute for orange candle stub)

I do not have an orange candle, so I use a small, gnarled little nub of carrot. The symbolism makes me laugh. I scratch his name into it with a needle, as instructed.

Burn the witch, this man's followers had screamed.

I light the candle. Through the glass pane of the door, the cat watches the flame flicker.

A week later, after days of being so glued to the television that Mackerel bonds with the news anchors on CNN, he loses the election.

It wasn't the spell, of course. Sometimes good things just happen.

Men accused of sexual violence have in recent years co-opted the femicidal history of the witch hunt to their own ends. It is he who is being accused without basis: not, as witches were, because of their failure to adhere to a patriarchal system, but from greedy malevolence: the evil women wish to topple him, for their own ends.

Now he is toppled.

It is getting cold, and the sun sits low in the sky. Perhaps it is this new chill in the air that brings Mackerel back to me, as I lie in bed reading. She has started curling up next to me again, puddling and purring. I am relieved, because it has been several weeks since I have seen her do either. She even begins to sit on my lap, a rare honour.

It is here that she settles on 13 November. For three or four years after the Paris attacks, this day never slipped by unnoticed. I would always find myself revisiting the city in my memory: the darkened, empty streets; the barricaded bars; running through the *quartier* past the trucks and trucks of soldiers being unloaded on to the Place de la Bastille; the sirens. That end-of-the-world feeling: pure, undiluted terror.

I would avoid thinking about how close we had come. How a series of seemingly insignificant decisions – to go to bed in the afternoon and oversleep, to decide to change our dining plans and walk slightly further into town – could well have marked the difference between living and dying. Instead, I thought of those who had not been so lucky, and the families they left behind.

This year, though, I forget the anniversary. Or at least, I am consciously unaware of the significance of the date. Yet I spend most of the day in bed with the cat, which I suppose says something.

In the pocket of my Burberry trench coat, there was a small orange that I had picked up that morning. As we sat in the bar, not knowing whether they were coming to shoot us, too, I reached in with my hand and felt its cold, waxy rind.

I was fourteen when I first saw Paris. My mother took me, though I didn't know how she afforded it at the time. She always seemed to find a way, was a marvel at making things happen on very little income. In my teenage years, I became used to the sight of her calculations on the backs of brown envelopes. Single mothers are financial magicians.

Penniless trips to Paris are part of our family's history. Shortly after they were married, my parents had gone there using the coupons that you got on the back of boxes of washing powder. They had stayed in Montmartre, and the photographs they took – on a Nikon EM, using black-and-white film, printed in a smaller format than your usual four-by-six – fascinated me as a child. It seemed to be a city that existed in the past, a place of gargoyles and statues, dark against the pale sky and chalky white cathedral domes, of dimly lit bars and rain-soaked cobbles and my mother and father looking young and very beautiful in their long wool coats and scarves.

My mother and I stayed in Montmartre, too, because I didn't want to stay at Disneyland.

Instead, we found a little hotel. It was that classic French sort of hotel: patterned frilled curtains in toile de Jouy and a matching bedspread, a little poky entrance under a small glass dome. I loved it, and I loved the streets surrounding it, which we walked while my mother told me about the artists who had lived and worked there, including the cat-loving Suzanne Valadon, whom everybody knew as Renoir's dancer but who was a great artist in her own right, and the Chat Noir theatre, which became their haunt. An artist sketched our portraits in soft pencil that blurred and smudged in transit to become Impressionistic, just as my memories are: the square in the rain with its shimmering cobbles.

It was the Paris that tourists see, but it was enough to convince me that I needed to be there. *Art matters here,* I thought. *I want to be where art matters.*

I ask my mother for her memories of the trip, and she tells me that it was partly funded by a charity for child carers. She said I refused to go to the support group, but they still contributed to a holiday for me. In doing so, they showed me a city, and taught me to want what I thought I couldn't have: A Big Life.

It's coming on Christmas, to quote Joni Mitchell. I've always felt that her song 'River' captured the melancholy of the season, a slightly shamefaced desire to skate away from it all. I love Christmas, but its cosy emphasis on togetherness has a tendency to cast less-than-ideal family circumstances into sharp relief. For my entire adult life, I have spent the festive season going from pillar to post in order to try and see everyone, a consequence of the divorce and my brother living in a care home.

This year, we also plan to visit family on my husband's side, and a friend who is unable to return to France offers to look after the cat. But the headlines are full of speculation about Christmas being cancelled, and so I start to plan a backup Christmas that is just my husband, Mackerel and I.

'A kitten's first Christmas is such a special time,' I am told by a neighbour. And I think: *She's a cat.* But all the same, I'd prefer not to leave her.

Four years after our mother–daughter trip to Paris, I moved there in the middle of a heatwave, to be an au pair for a family in the 16th arrondissement. The first evening, I stopped weeping long enough to take the Metro into the city.

All day, I had been plagued by the persistent feeling that my clothes were all wrong, and not only because of the heat. I had never felt attractive in my teens, so it came as a surprise to me that, in Paris, men seemed to think me beautiful. Just eighteen, I walked alone through a tangle of streets on the Left Bank and was told repeatedly that I was '*charmante*', the meaning of which I would look up in my dictionary, later, in my tiny attic room. I had spent my adolescence assessing myself through male eyes, but it was only in Paris that I was able, for the first time, to take strength and succour from that gaze and, in some ways, to begin to construct myself as an adult woman. Perhaps it is different for young women now – I do hope so – but uncomfortable though it is, I only really began to see myself once I was desired.

I had been a sister and a daughter and a carer, a good student and even a girlfriend. This was different. In the dusk,

I felt alive with the knowledge that no one in the world knew where I was in that moment, and drunk with the realisation that I had something that men wanted. I walked into a dark bar and sat at the counter. All the windows were open, and a warm breeze wafted in from the narrow street. I could smell the buckwheat batter cooking on the hot plate of the crêperie opposite, mingling with perfume and cigarette smoke and hot pavement. I ordered a glass of wine and drank it slowly.

I opened the notebook I had just bought, an exercise book covered with Magritte's dream clouds, and as I sat there, I felt another body hovering against mine. Not touching, but close enough that my skin could feel him. He had his back to me, showed no outward sign of having seen me at all. But I felt it: a frisson.

Cats hate the smell of citrus. It is for this reason that, when we brought Mackerel home, I sprayed the walls with orange oil. She had taken to trying to climb the woodchip wallpaper and it was coming off in little ribbons beneath her claws. Though it would need replacing anyway, due to the damp having caused it to peel, I took these measures to deter her, the air of the flat thickening with the sharp, sweet scent.

I could see it as a twist of fate that my first paid employment after leaving home for Paris would be looking after a child who had additional needs, undiagnosed but plain, at least, to me. I could say something trite about trying to run away from your intended path. But as with a friend who laments that she keeps choosing the same narcissistic men, maybe it's as much a case of them choosing you. Perhaps my face, my demeanour, carries a message. The mothers see it. Men, I think, can see it too.

I am good at care work, but I failed with this particular child. I was fond of both brothers, but the younger was simply adorable: sweet, bespectacled and highly intelligent. The older brother, perhaps because of the attention that was lavished upon his sibling by their parents when they were around, was a ball of rage. He kicked, bit, and spat at me. '*Ce n'est pas gentil,*' I used to say. 'It is not kind.'

I did my best. I made the quiche, I picked them up from school, I brought them home, I gave them the quiche, I took them back to school, then three hours later I went back to fetch them. I did this every day, for a room in the servants' attic and seventy-five euros a week. I was very unhappy: I had come to Paris looking for freedom, but found myself instead in a domestic prison with an unhappy child who was crying out for love that I – depleted from my own life experiences and essentially still a child myself – was unable to give.

Furthermore, I found the father creepy. The only shower was in their en suite, separated from the bedroom where he would lie on the bed by a rubber concertina that was scarcely a door, behind which I would stand, naked and furious, hating him.

I dig out the Magritte notebook and turn to some of the earliest pages, written in the autumn of my arrival in Paris. I would sit and write in it in the Jardin du Luxembourg near the statue of George Sand (another writer who loved cats; it is said that Chopin's Waltz in F Major was inspired by the sound of her cat, Valdeck, scampering across the piano's keyboard) and the trees under which Gwen John would sleep with her cat, Tiger.

I don't know if I wanted to be a writer by that point. I would never have thought to talk about this writing to anyone, or even to examine my reasons for doing it. After my year in France, I was to go to a prestigious university to study law. I had chosen this career path because it guaranteed financial stability, without understanding the unhappiness it would bring.

These days, when I write, I try to distil emotion on the page with honesty and clarity. This is not the case with my Paris notebook. Much of it feels overwrought and derivative, refracted through a prism of cultural reference points invoking doomed romance or fraught affairs undertaken by adults. As a result, it is excruciating to read. As we age, we are supposed to accumulate at least a little wisdom, so to be confronted with our guileless younger selves is mortifying. I feel like writing on the front:

IN THE EVENT OF MY DEATH,
PLEASE BURN THIS NOTEBOOK.

Maybe I sound unkind to my younger self, whose only crime was to be lost and earnest in a country that was not her own. Yet I cannot bring myself to burn it. In it, I describe a dream in which I'm getting ready to be married to my then-boyfriend in a black veiled 'widow's hat'. The dream ends with my fleeing the ceremony and scaling the city walls, which were as tall as a house, to escape the groom.

As metaphors go, my unconscious wasn't exactly subtle.

Another failure of memory: in my notebook, I express disgust at being looked at. I write that I hate making eye contact with strangers in the street or on the Metro. And yet I also write that I want to be told that I am beautiful, but – naturally – only by someone who I think is beautiful, too.

In the Decembers of my childhood, we made clove oranges, the fruit so large we could barely hold them in our small, fat hands as we pushed the spices into their skins. Christmas is always a little sad because it is a tradition that is steeped in the past, and so lends itself so easily to thoughts of loss, but in this year of mass disease and death and separation from family, it feels even more so.

My sister-in-law, who also adopted a kitten during the first lockdown, is considering not bothering with a tree this year, as she is sure that her rambunctious cat will simply topple it. This seems, to me, a drastic course of action. Everything is so miserable that I feel we must have a tree as soon as possible.

I try and remember how the cats interacted with the tree when I was growing up and don't recall anything too disastrous happening (I do remember tying the tree to the ceiling). Nor did they seem interested in eating the pine needles, which the internet keeps telling me are poisonous. It seems to me that in those days, we didn't fret about our cats so much – we put our faith in their survival instincts, and generally that faith paid off. This is what I strive to do with Mackerel. Besides, since she fell from the bookcase, she hasn't been much of a climber.

Still, I order a large bag of dried orange slices to hang from the lowest branches as a deterrent. Just in case.

Two reasons why I stuck it out as an au pair for so long, despite the man who listened to me shower and the violence of his son:

1) I worried about the children, particularly the elder. They needed someone to be there for them, and I felt guilty at the thought of leaving them.
2) My room had a view of the Eiffel Tower. I would watch it at night, alone in my room, as the lights switched from static to shimmering and back again.

Shortly before I returned home for Christmas, it snowed just as night was falling. They were the sort of big, fat flakes that you'd get at home in the mountains, coming thick and fast like a blizzard in a storybook, swirling around the lit-up tower and the peaked rooftops of all the other attics that stood between us. As clichés went, it was almost too much.

But I was eighteen and I had come to that city from a small place in search of a big life. The ridiculous cinematic view served as a reminder that I was in a place where things *happened*; that there was an existence beyond being this family's miserable, quiche-making skivvy.

The first thing I do with the orange slices is make a wreath for the front door. I am well-practised at this because I was once sent to write an article about wreath-making as part of my first graduate job, as an editorial assistant on a small online magazine.

My friends and I had all graduated into a recession. There

is a photograph of me that day – almost a decade ago, now – in cap and gown, and in it I am holding up my unemployment booklet from the Jobcentre. I'm smiling through the fear, but I remember how anxious I was: there were no jobs, and I had no family money or savings, and I was reeling from the previous autumn's street attack, terrified of dark evenings and strung out from disrupted, nightmare-filled nights.

Despite the best attempts of some, I never felt shame about claiming welfare. I have my mother to thank for that, I think. As a single parent to a disabled child, she had been part of the system for years, but never allowed it to grind her down. Though I had seen her weep on the phone to the benefits people and worry about how she'd pay for school shoes, she also created the warmest, happiest home for us. It doesn't take much: food, music turned up loud, dancing, laughter, art, love.

When I finally got a job and phoned up to inform the benefits office, the woman thought I was joking.

The job was in the west of the city, where some of the richest people live. The commute took almost two hours, often longer because I had to keep getting off the train, unable to breathe and convinced I was about to die. I felt, as I often had since leaving home, that I was walking a tightrope between two worlds: in one, I was mixing with people with unimaginable wealth, privilege, and connections; in another, I lived precariously, with no safety net and no resources to make a writing life possible.

Everyone else at the wreath-making workshop had paid hundreds of pounds for the privilege. Most of them were older women, but there were two girls my age. I remember that one was wearing a pair of black velvet ballet pumps. Each was embroidered, in shining gold thread, with the face of a cat, and had a small gold heel. I remember thinking they were the sort of shoes that a princess might wear.

'I love your shoes,' I said to her. 'Where did you get them from?'

The princess was from another world. At the end of the class, I watched her get into a chauffeur-driven car with tinted windows to be taken back there. Then I began the long journey home through the bowels of the city, relieved that the dusk had not yet turned to darkness, meaning that I would not have to hurry home breathless with terror, convinced I was being followed. When I got there, I looked up the shoes. They cost more than my rent.

In the midst of a plague, I make the wreath the way I learned that day. I have no eucalyptus or expensive materials. I am using mostly branches that I have foraged from the neighbourhood: olive, rosemary, ivy, pine. I also know that this time no one from my family will see it, except through a screen, but to make and hang it feels more important than ever. I pierce holes in the orange flesh and tie the rounds to the frame so that they nestle there like dried suns amidst the green, promising health, survival.

On top of my wardrobe, in a box embossed with gold

text, are the shoes. I had bought them when I sold my first book.

We always have a real tree, ever since the first Christmas that we were together. Neither of us had much money – this was the year I graduated – and so we went to a cheap shop and bought a little white plastic Christmas tree for the kitchen. The sight of it made me sad, and I think he could tell, because the next day I came home and in my bedroom he had placed a real live tree, fully decorated with blue and silver decorations. It was one of the many ways he showed me that I had found a good man.

My husband carries the tree home against the backdrop of a blazing afternoon sunset, their silhouettes merging against the furious pink and orange of the sky. I had advocated for a small tree, mindful that the cat might try and climb it, but as usual, we reach the Christmas tree-sellers who set up shop in the car park at the local pub and my husband is overtaken by excitement. It is as though he has some subconscious rule that the tree has to be taller than he is, harking back to being dwarfed by the festive firs of childhood, and as he is six foot three, this always means we end up with a gigantic pine in the living room.

When we bring it in, Mackerel is excited by this strange, looming object with its new smells. She sniffs it curiously.

'Soon you'll be climbing trees outside,' I say. We tie it to the wall, to be safe.

There was one Christmas – I think it was the year I lived in Paris, or perhaps the following year – when I returned home in the days leading up to it and there was still no tree. My mother hadn't been able to afford one, and though she had made an effort to decorate in other ways, stringing lights around the ceiling beams, and holly and ivy on the mantlepiece and on top of the picture frames, its absence was nonetheless plain.

'We'll just have to find one,' I told her, 'but we'll need a strong man.'

'What are you planning . . .?' She looked perturbed. 'Don't ask any more questions,' I said.

Jacob came down the mountain that evening, so I wouldn't have to walk up alone in the dark. His parents had expressed concern that he would be shot by a farmer. 'They're acting like they're the Forestry Commission,' he said.

'This is why you shouldn't have said anything,' I said.

We wore dark clothing, though it scarcely mattered. The track up the mountain is only really used in daytime, by locals trying to avoid the tourists entering the village by the main road. Other than a few houses dotting the landscape – some of them long-abandoned derelict cottages – there are very few other signs of habitation. The road is lined by forest and has few landmarks, save that it passes through the middle of an abandoned quarry. It is here that, as a child, I stood and looked down into the bright turquoise waters of a lake that was once a hole and saw a glistening silver creature twisting and shimmering, too large to be any kind of fish I knew.

I knew this landscape intimately, from childhood. Which is how I knew that a little further along the road, which has no street lights (we were using a torch to guide us), is a paddock containing a number of small pines no taller than a man.

'I'll climb down,' Jacob said. 'You keep watch.' He scrambled over the wall and jumped down to the field below. I beamed the torch in his direction, then back and forth like a searchlight until I found him. 'What about this one?'

'Looks great,' I said, and he began to saw.

I'll never forget the look on my brother's face when Jacob carried the tree indoors and set it down in the corner of the living room. The mission was worth it for that smile. 'Christmas tree! Christmas tree!' he said, over and over, jumping up and down with excitement. After Jacob left, my mother and I strung it with twinkle lights and baubles and lametta so it shone. We placed the angel – a childhood doll of my mother's, which, when I was small, we'd kitted out in a little dress and fairy wings – on the top.

When I thanked Jacob, he seemed faintly embarrassed.

I still bring it up, every Christmas: 'Remember when you stole us a tree?'

It remains one of the nicest gifts I've ever received.

Since my mother sold my childhood home, the Christmas tree decorations reside in my flat. Her rented place is too small for a tree, and my brother's care home have their own decorations. Unpacking the ornaments is always a nostalgic exercise, even more so this year. It is coming up to a year since I last saw my brother, and I am conscious that I should have taken my chances in the summer, when things had opened up – my terror of infecting him had kept me away. Missing him is a feeling that I have had to place in a tightly closed box.

My brother is undemonstrative, so in the past it was hard to know whether he missed us or not. But then one Easter Sunday my mother didn't come, and my brother cried so hard that when one of his carers phoned, it sounded as though she had been weeping too, at the sight of it. It was a chain reaction: my mother took the call and left the art gallery that she was in, bawling.

The next day, my father got in the car and drove straight over. We never made that mistake again.

When it becomes apparent that we won't be able to travel this Christmas, and that we won't see anyone over the festive period, my mother sobs down the phone.

'At least you can be with him,' I say. 'He'll be so happy to be with you.'

I'm doing fine, I think. A quiet Christmas in the city: it will be lovely.

I am cooking and listening to Ella and Louis when she starts singing 'Have Yourself a Merry Little Christmas', and I find myself winded by the lyrics, which I had never listened to properly before, and which speak of separation, and looking forward to a Christmas when we can all be together again.

'Until then, we'll have to muddle through somehow,' Ella sings. 'So have yourself a merry little Christmas now.'

I have to take the pan off the heat, as I can no longer see the stew.

Mackerel spends hours with the tree. She won't climb it, but she sits on the windowsill and rests her front paws in its branches, peering through the needles like a pine marten. Undeterred by the orange slices, she bats the baubles hanging from the bottom branches, tearing the fluffy guts from the felt narwhal ornament that has become her favourite toy. And she sleeps curled up underneath it, next to the trunk, enjoying the shelter it offers.

Marooned in the city, away from our loved ones, we somehow manage to stay cheerful. We drink martinis, listen to my 'Merry Fucking Christmas' playlist, and play Scrabble. My longing for a child is still acute, but sitting next to it is a kernel of hope. By next Christmas, this whole thing might be over. There might be a baby, I think, or I might be pregnant. We should enjoy this time together, just the two of us – and Mackerel, of course.

Then comes the news of a vaccine. We pop corks; tears are shed. It is only now, with a positive development, that it dawns on me that we have spent many, many months without a clear end in sight, grappling with a disease with no inoculation or cure. Somehow, I have managed to stay sane.

As long as you don't count the fact that I've channelled all my difficult emotions into the care of a small, furry cat.

A month after the Paris attacks, my mother came to London for Christmas. I wasn't up to travelling, I told her. My brother was spending the day at my dad's, and my then-boyfriend, now-husband would be going to see his parents and siblings.

The orange still sat in my trench coat pocket, petrifying. I refused to throw it out, having come to believe that it was keeping me alive.

I was not well. The sound of a helicopter hovering above the house – a common occurrence in my part of the city – sent me running to the bathroom, the only room without windows, where I cowered, curled up on the floor. I know now that the noise must have reminded me of that night, of the feeling of being in a warzone, under attack, in the same way that sirens left me jittery. I understood what it meant to be triggered, because after the street attack, I had had several months of therapy, and understanding the psychology of post-traumatic stress had been crucial to my recovery. I knew that the traumatised mind can struggle to sort memories properly, which means that you continue to live with the trauma. It's as though a part of you never left: when triggered, you're back to being inside that night. You're back running through the streets of Paris, past restaurants barricaded with frightened people inside, past the trucks unloading all the soldiers – the only other people out in the open, and they're wearing body armour – wondering if the gunmen are coming for you.

It had only been a month, and I was in denial about the PTSD coming back. *It's natural to be a bit jittery after a scare like that,* I told myself. I just needed to take it easy at home, avoid public transport and bars and restaurants for a little while (a huge error, I would later learn).

Christmas dinner at the local pub with my mother should be manageable, though, I thought.

On the day, the atmosphere was as festive as an inn from a Dickens adaptation. A fire roared next to a huge tree, and the bar was full of people who had finished their post-prandial walks and had stopped in for drinks. As I entered,

I made a note of the exits. They would probably come in through the main door, and shoot up the bar area first, before moving on to the dining room. If we were to live, we would have to flee via the garden, assuming they didn't have us surrounded. It took all my strength to walk over to our table and sit down.

It's hard to explain, in retrospect, that I truly believed that I would die that day, that this Christmas lunch would be my last meal, but that is how it was, and how it would be for the next year. I couldn't focus on what my mother was saying. I couldn't move my eyes away from the doors. I ate a small bite of each thing on my plate, and stopped. They boxed it all up for me, but I could hardly stand to look at it.

I put my hand in my pocket and gave the rotten orange a squeeze.

Bad things happen to me and my family: this is one of my 'core beliefs'. Dr N, the clinical psychologist, and I identified it in the trauma-focused therapy I was given on the NHS in the aftermath of my attack. I was only supposed to be given six sessions, but Dr N extended it for almost a whole year, and in doing so, I believe, saved my life. Identifying my core beliefs was part of the work of trying to unpick the night that I was strangled and process my memories. I remember saying the words out loud, the pain of that admission: it was physical.

We discussed how my childhood and my brother's diagnosis may have affected me; how the belief that he would die from a seizure fitted into this worldview that I had developed. Divorce, my father's diagnosis with MS when I was a teenager, school bullying: all had contributed to this idea that my life was a waiting room for tragedy, that things inevitably fall apart.

Each family has its shocks and its losses and its heartbreaks. I think that, in my case, I was already vulnerable, having been a worrier since I was very small. A family history of anxiety and depression undoubtedly coalesced with some of the things that happened to me early in life to make me the perfect candidate for post-traumatic stress.

I suspect, had a stranger not tried to strangle me to death, I'd have muddled through life with some minor melancholia.

It was important that I understood that the things that had happened to me did not make me an unfit candidate for love, nor did they make me incapable of giving love.

'Just because you think something doesn't make it true,' my mother always said, encapsulating cognitive behavioural therapy's entire *raison d'être*.

Until I dispensed with the demands of chronology, I did not know how to tell this story. As Elena Ferrante writes in *Frantumaglia*, 'We are tornadoes that pick up fragments

with the most varied historical and biological origins.'
Memories are fragments. The way we remember is never
linear. Recollections blend and blur and swirl together, can
be interrupted by other pictures, other threads. Motifs and
symbols emerge: cats, or oranges, or eggs, or poppets. With
trauma, establishing order can be vital.

Dr N and I wrote down what happened that night and
went over it again and again, adding and embellishing as
more detail emerged. The walk across the darkened park.
The man asking for a cigarette. The realising there were
more of them. The hands around my neck.

This is how to file the memory properly, Dr N said. Then
I read it to myself, then to a tape recorder. I listened to my
trauma over and over until it ceased to affect me at all.
Together, we consigned it to the past.

I believe that post-traumatic stress is the closest humans
come to time travel, and after the long, hard work of therapy,
we were able to seal the portal. It's just a memory now, like
the others.

Until it isn't.

The solstice always makes me think of the year when I was
ten or eleven, and I did a snow spell I found in a book.
Three days later, on Christmas Eve, it came down in a blizzard that saw us running outside in the dark to twirl and

swirl with it. The next morning, it was three feet deep. And all, I thought naively, because of me. My cat Jessie brought us a dead robin as a gift. Her sacrifice was laid lovingly on the doorstep, the red of its breast fierce against the snow.

There's a melancholy to the festive season that causes the mind to turn to all the past Christmases, and the loved ones who are no longer with us, or simply the surprisingly painful knowledge that you will never be a child again, and don't have a child through whose eyes you can see it anew.

I thought I would be sad on Christmas Eve listening to Nine Lessons and Carols without my mother there, but instead I raise a glass to her, smiling. I have made martinis and anchovy cheese puffs, and these small comforts help.

My husband cooks a ham that evening, which we were able to obtain after several failed attempts. With it, he serves a blood orange and fennel salad.

Mackerel loves the present-opening in the morning. From my stepmother, she receives a little knitted ball with a bell inside, and from my aunt, a hand-knitted blanket as soft as fur. From us, an array of toys and treats and tuna.

But first we leave her and walk through the quiet streets as the sun rises. The day is cold and bright, perfect weather for my husband's swim. I watch him with the other families, their loved ones' figures black silhouettes against a pearly winter sky as they make their way down the jetty to the freezing water. I have a hipflask of rum for when he comes out, electrified.

At home, we eat salmon and eggs to the radio; a choir singing 'In the Bleak Midwinter', one of my favourite carols. I can see why we feast and celebrate at this point of the year, bringing light to the darkness. I roast a guinea fowl with all the trimmings while listening to Tom Waits channelling a hooker in Minneapolis, Prince singing of loneliness, drinking banana daiquiris 'til he's blind, Shane MacGowan and Kirsty MacColl in the drunk tank, their hedonism making our cosy, low-key Christmas feel sedate in comparison.

After lunch, Mackerel devours the leftovers. 'She has expensive taste,' I say.

As it turns out, the cat's first Christmas is very special.

Returning for Christmas the year I left home only made me realise how unhappy I was as an au pair, and how constraining it felt to be continuing the care work I thought I had left behind. Still, I boarded the flight back to Paris in early January and wept quietly for the entire journey, turning my face to the darkened sky through the airplane window so that the girl sitting next to me, who was around the same age, couldn't see. It wasn't until baggage collection – when my cheap, burst-open suitcase came around the carousel, alongside all my ejected underwear – that I abandoned all pretence of holding it together. The girl, who introduced herself as Maggie, came up to me and asked, with a certain amount of shyness, if there was anything she could do to help. And so, together, we boarded the train to where she was staying near the Jardin du Luxembourg, and from there she helped me get a taxi.

'Did you know I was crying the whole time on the plane?' I asked her, a week later, when I took her out for a drink to say thank you for her kindness.

'I had no idea,' she said.

I suspected that, in her very English way, she had wanted to afford me my privacy. This is how we became friends.

Maggie is now thirty-eight and tired of being asked if she is freezing her eggs. She lives on her own in a cottage and has a man who she sees on weekends. She adopted her own pandemic kitten, Orlando, not long after we got Mackerel. Orlando, now four months old, is a marmalade kitten with a beautiful white bib. I had assumed he was named after the Woolf novel (Maggie is a literature graduate), but in fact his name was taken from a series of children's books that ran from 1938–1972. When Orlando first arrived, Maggie tells me that he hid under the bed for two days. But since then he has very much made himself at home. In the photos she sends me, he looks blissfully happy, sprawled out on the bed, snoozing.

In early January, I returned to my Parisian life of childcare and drudgery: school, quiche, school, ironing, school, home-work, repeat. And while doing this, I was bitten and kicked and insulted. I never responded angrily. I felt only pity for this child. All the same, he was not my brother. I didn't have love to make up for the harder parts.

I have a vivid memory of this time of standing in an immaculate park in a well-heeled neighbourhood, the frosted ground solid beneath my feet, and feeling the most desperate, painful loneliness. The parts of the day where I wasn't working were spent in solitude, waiting until I was needed. I would try and write during these times, but the dullness of my existence didn't lend itself well to creativity. I had been to a writing group upstairs at Shakespeare and Company – a famous bookshop where itinerant writers sleep among the stacks – but so far, I hadn't read out any of my work. I sat and listened to other people read theirs, my eyes on Kitty, the white cat curled up in the corner, as I wondered how many terrible novels she had sat through over the years.

Sometimes it takes seeing your situation through the eyes of another for you to realise how bad it is. Maggie had already witnessed my meltdown at the airport. A couple of weeks later, my friend Shakes arrived for a weekend. She took in the servants' quarters, the terrible pay, the lack of free time, and the uncomfortable bathroom situation, and said, baldly: 'Well, this is a bit shit, isn't it?'

'It is,' I said. 'It really is.'

Things have turned very bad. In the aftermath of festivities, cases of the virus are rising exponentially; deaths, too. The old fear is back, reminding me of the beginning of all this. Outside, everything is grey and flat.

I have been working on an article about the mental health toll of the virus on medical staff since March. It keeps being pushed back, and pushed back, and each time I have needed to do more research and conduct more interviews. I am haunted by the things I have been told: how it feels to see the person you are caring for slowly drown while their loved ones watch through a screen; how an ICU nurse lay on the floor, wishing she could die. The psychologist I interview tells me that healthcare workers are developing complex-PTSD from sustained, repeated exposure to trauma. C-PTSD is usually seen in veterans, or victims of child abuse.

I have been living with these stories for too long. I am having nightmares. I want to get them on the page, tell the story, and move on.

But there has been some good news: my husband is called for his vaccine. He has to go up to the hospital to get it, and it is the first time he has seen his colleagues in almost a year. He sends me a picture of them masked up, in the waiting room. It is only as the weight of my fear for him lifts that I realise the load that I have been carrying.

Sometimes, when he leaves the house, I catch myself wondering if it will be the last time. Some calamity will befall him and this will be it, the final words. And so I say, 'I love you,' like a maniac. A bit like a child, I have always feared abandonment more than I fear any harm coming to myself.

When I was very ill, I was convinced everyone I loved would die. I got better, but the traces are still there: the accelerated heartbeat, the sharp spike of fear. The scene plays out in a reel before my eyes: the doorbell, the police officer's grave face, how I collapse on the floor. It spins around and around, like a kitten trapped in the drum of a washing machine, bloody and tragic and morbid.

After Shakes left Paris, I broke up with my long-distance boyfriend mercilessly via telephone and promptly forgot all about him. I also vowed to leave my job.

I find out that my brother is not on the vaccine priority list, despite being profoundly disabled and living in a care home – both risk factors for hospitalisation and death from Covid-19. No considerations have been made for how difficult he would be to ventilate or keep calm in a hospital setting, nor for the risk he might pose to medical staff.

When I speak to his care workers, they are in shock.

They have had their vaccinations and are baffled that the boys have not.

I spend a week on the phone, calling everyone I can think of. I contact the health board and disability charities and Public Health and politicians. I email my brother's local doctor and ask what they are doing with their spare vaccines – couldn't they just do the boys? There are only five of them.

This is what it's like, loving a vulnerable person. You have to become a full-time activist.

My rage at the injustice of this decision triggers something in me. I feel fury, and sorrow, as though I am only now processing all the times we have had to fight for him over the years to ensure he gets the care he deserves. I realise that I have been keeping a lid on my fear. Even before the pandemic, I was scared for him. There were seizures that ended in hospitalisation, late-night phone calls to my mother that went unanswered, that left me expecting the worst. (Once, in the small hours, I became so convinced that something had happened to him that I begged a family friend from the next valley to drive over in person and check, as my calls were ringing out. He had indeed had a seizure. The banging on the door woke my mother, alerting her to the fact that he was dangerously cold and needed an ambulance.)

But since last March, the fear has been a constant simmer, and to have been given the hope of protection only to have it taken away breaks something in me. I am frantic, and when I am not frantic, all I want to do is sleep.

When I'm resting in bed, Mackerel always comes through to see me. Never a lap cat, I suspect she is using me for my body heat when she drapes herself across me. But I need comfort, and whatever the reason for this new increased proximity, it is welcome. She sleeps there, sometimes for hours, her body vibrating, letting out the occasional sigh, her ears twitching as the sun sinks yet again below the buildings and the sky changes from blue to darker blue, but, because we are in the city, never, thankfully, black.

Feeding her is what gets me out of bed in the morning. She is always so happy to see me.

I spent a couple of weeks plotting my departure from Parisian servitude. I had been planning on handing in my notice to Madame in a calm and measured fashion, so that I could work out the rest of the month and find a new place to live. Say goodbye to the boys properly.

It didn't happen like that. Apparently I had used the wrong setting on the iron for the boys' Petit Bateau polo necks, and had caused them to become misshapen. She summoned me to their wardrobe so that she could show me, like a person shoving a cat's face in its own mess. They looked the same as before.

I tried to imagine my own mother, with her lackadaisical approach to ironing, which she often hid, and her refusal to pair up socks (if you needed some, you went to the 'sock bag' and were on your own), getting so angry about something like this, and I thought: *I am done.*

I explained that I couldn't do this anymore, and was told that I would need to leave immediately.

Which is how I ended up with all my worldly goods piled up into a shopping trolley borrowed from the nearest supermarket, making my way through the fanciest area of Paris to a friend's house, to sleep on her floor.

The day after my article about trauma is published, it snows, and I feel, suddenly, free. Objectively speaking, I am far from it: the strict lockdown continues, but there is something childishly liberating about snow and how it causes us to abandon our usual dutiful days. Snow trumps everything.

Mackerel is fascinated: she sits on the windowsill watching the flakes tumble and fall, not sure what to make of it all.

We decide to go up to the Heath for a walk. On the way up there, I see an old woman standing at her window, holding up her cat so that the cat can see the flurries. It is hard to interpret the cat's facial expression, but the woman looks happy. Look! I imagine her saying. Look at the snow! I smile and wave.

When we reach the Heath, it is as though the fever has gone and the whole city is celebrating. Adults and children pelt each other with snowballs. Crowds are careening down the hill, some on beautiful handmade wooden sledges, and some on whatever they can find: tea trays and dustbin lids. In the woodland, the cries of laughter vanish and all is still, the only sound our feet crunching as we walk through the frosted trees, and the occasional soft landing of snow from a branch that could take no more weight. I have seen this landscape in all seasons, but perhaps this is the most beautiful. It is certainly the most fleeting. Soon it will be brown and slushy, its untouched icing sugar surface only a memory, like all the ephemeral snow days that came before it.

After fleeing my position, I stayed with an American friend who was also an au pair but had the luxury of a self-contained flat and the use of a car, though it was 'a stick', something she complained about when she was driving us to her favourite gyros place, which she pronounced 'giro', as in cheque. She was older than me, a college graduate, and she and her friend had baptised me into American drinking culture: games of beer pong, flip cup and power hour. We had little in common, except that we liked going out at night to meet Frenchmen who then took us to house parties. Sarah was on a break from her college boyfriend, who she would later marry. My enduring memory of her is of her sitting on a dawn Metro train back to the 16th arrondissement, drunk and wearing a pink cowboy hat.

I set about finding a new family. I was adamant that I wouldn't be an au pair again – the hours were too long and the 'pocket money' too low. I wanted time and space to write and explore and actually live in the city, not the half-existence of a kept member of household staff. So I resolved to find an arrangement that traded a room or an apartment for a certain number of babysitting hours, but where my time outside of that was my own. I scoured the small ads and found Aurelie.

I liked Aurelie immediately, because her house was a shit tip. She had just had another baby, and although it was a big apartment, it wasn't big enough for all of her six children and Aurelie and her husband, Bernard, a doctor. I'm not talking about a small amount of mess, either. It was as though a laundry bomb, a toy bomb, a paperwork bomb, and a crockery bomb had all exploded at once. There were children's beds in almost every room, and a rabbit in the kitchen. Aurelie and Bernard lived in what was essentially a cupboard with a platform bed built into it. I fell in love with it, and them, immediately.

She explained to me that my duties were simple: on weekdays, I would collect the three youngest children – aged seven, five and three – from school at around 4pm, take them home or to the park, give them a snack, help them with their homework, keep an eye on the older two and sometimes the baby, and be done by six. That was all, bar the occasional evening of babysitting. In exchange, I got my attic room with a separate entrance, and though I'd still need to use the shower downstairs, it was self-contained. I think she thought it was a big ask, because she seemed a bit surprised by my emphatic yes.

The snow is melting. A friend who works in a hospital says that they are vaccinating friends and family with spare doses to avoid waste and that I should get down there the next day. The current advice is that any woman who is trying for a baby or is planning to do so should wait for three months after her jab, which, when you account for the second dose, would mean a delay of six months before we could begin to start trying to conceive.

My husband thinks that I should have the injection, but all I can think about is a baby. The longing hasn't gone away – if anything, it has become especially acute during the winter months – but the ongoing public health crisis has stopped us taking any decisive action. At times, I feel as though I am worrying unnecessarily: so many friends have either announced their pregnancies or given birth to a child. In the time that I have been thinking, questioning, worrying, oscillating, some have had two.

I walk in circles around the park, on the phone to my best

friend, who is in between busy hospital shifts. She gently advises me to get immunised, but my desire to be a mother is ravenous and primal. It swallows all logical argument.

To go would involve a trip to the other side of the city, alone. I'll have a panic attack, I think, and there will be no one there to help me.

I decide not to go. I go and have coffee with a writer for a prestigious American magazine in a freezing park, instead. We speak of art and books and living in the city, and I am cheered by the conversation.

The next morning, I come to my senses. It is the weekend. I go down to the hospital, but it's a no-go. 'You should have come yesterday, it was a free-for-all,' the nurse says. Since then, they have been told off by management. All the spare doses were to be thrown away.

I have been managing well. This is what I tell myself, and I believe it. But it's the darkest part of winter now, and we are all like icebergs stranded from one another, forbidden from meeting indoors, while outdoors we are only permitted to meet in pairs. There is nowhere to go and nothing to do; even the ponds are closed, so my husband is unable to swim through it. Gathering around the firepit in the garden, where we entertained friends before Christmas, and where my husband discovered the joy of toasted marshmallows for the first time, making a face like a little boy at his first taste of their fondant centres, has lost its appeal. I go to see my friend and we stand in a blizzard behind some public toilets while she smokes, our faces stinging as we try to converse across the wind.

I have not known sorrow like this for a long time. There is the eternal conflict: the desire for a child when the world is going mad. Not to mention the fact that I myself have been mad, and fear that motherhood would send me there again. Could a traumatic birth retrigger my PTSD? Would I develop postnatal depression? It would not be fair to inflict that on a child, who deserves a happy life, a present mother.

Forward momentum feels impossible: we should leave the city, probably, in search of a more stable life, but we can't quite work out how. I was born here, it is where I feel I belong, and it is hard to know what the future will look like when all this is over and the world comes back to life. Like many others, we are in the grip of inertia.

There is the fact that this pandemic feels like the beginning of something, the opening strings of a catastrophic symphony that will only soar to greater heights: floods, wildfires, extreme weather, drought, a refugee crisis, more pandemics as a result of environmental carelessness, political chaos and extremism. There is the distance from my loved ones, and my powerlessness to keep them safe. The empty, echoing loneliness of a time without the joy that other people bring into our lives.

And there's the fact that I fear I am going back there,

into the hole, and that it could swallow all that is good and that somehow still remains.

I take to reading poetry every day: a sure sign that I am low. I come across 'February', by Margaret Atwood. It begins:

> Winter. Time to eat fat
> and watch hockey. In the pewter mornings, the cat,
> a black fur sausage with yellow
> Houdini eyes, jumps up on the bed and tries
> to get onto my head. It's his
> way of telling whether or not I'm dead.

I like the sense of hibernation and dormancy that Atwood evokes, then undercuts with the humorous description of the cat as a sausage. It reminds me of Mackerel, who will not leave me alone when I lie in bed feeling sorry for myself. She does not jump on my head, but instead nudges my face with her jowls. I never thought that it would be a cat that would help get me through what has so far been the loneliest time of my life. Winter is depressing, Atwood – another cat woman – seems to be saying, but take heart, because there will always be cats.

I find myself wondering how the cat women of the world are coping, whether they too are congratulating themselves on their furry companions, and whether the cats are congratulating themselves because they no longer have to share their humans' affections with countless other people.

The poem continues:

Cat, enough of your greedy whining
and your small pink bumhole.
Off my face! You're the life principle,
more or less, so get going
on a little optimism around here.
Get rid of death. Celebrate increase. Make it be spring.

I like that: the life principle. Perhaps having a baby would be the life principle, too.

Instead of seeing motherhood as an act that will only deprive me of freedom and sanity, a role of which I am unworthy, or the foolhardy choice of a person blind to the direction of world events, I need to find another way of framing it, if I am to do it. I need to find another way of transcribing the trauma that has been wrought upon my body without making myself a prisoner of it.

Ferrante says that 'honest writing forces itself to find words for those parts of our experience that are hidden and silent'.

I think of this when I am writing and I feel afraid of the consequences, when I shrink from the sneer of the proverbial male philosophy student who dismisses the work of women as therapy. I must force myself forward.

In the summer, my mother sent me a poem that she had written when she was pregnant with me. In it, she is walking down a street not far from where I live now, and stops at a fruit stall 'when the baby chose an orange'. She describes it, beautifully, as a 'cold, curved flame weighed in my hands'. I imagine her eating it on the pavement while looking at a shop window, just as she recounts in the poem. Me inside her. An us that, despite our physical distance, has never ceased to be.

Finally, we meet. In the freezing park, I cannot hug her, but I stand there holding her hands tightly in mine.

It's blood orange season, and my husband has bought a whole, big bag. He sits in the armchair and peels one, and I know what is coming. In a moment, he will place the peelings in a little pile on top of the record player and hand me a segment. I will eat it and the sour sunshine of its juice will fill my mouth, and I will think: I am eating an orange. Things could be worse.

VI

Spring

There was a time when I imagined that I would emerge from this pandemic-enforced period of isolation like a phoenix from the ashes: glowing, thin and well-rested, with a completed second novel under my arm and maybe even a baby on the way. Instead, I have enormous bags under my eyes, sallow skin, mad, unruly hair that is almost waist-length, and a cat on a lead.

In short, I may have become a witch.

Perhaps this is how witches are made. Something catastrophic happens – a plague, an act of violence, a broken heart, a lost child – and something inside a woman breaks. When a woman breaks, it usually means one thing: she starts to operate outside the norms that society expects of her. Perhaps she ceases to pay so much attention to her appearance, or abandons the accommodating sweetness she has performed since girlhood and instead gives herself over to fury, or resigns herself to a life of solitude, to pleasing herself rather than caring for others. One does not need to have lived through trauma to make these choices, of course, but trauma can facilitate them. There's a certain psychic liberation that comes from having faced death, a righteous anger that can free women from expectation. I see it in my friends who have had traumatic births; I felt it myself after I was attacked. It is how I found my feminism. Trauma often breeds rebellion.

In the film *Cat People* (1942), jealousy leads a woman to transform into a cat and attempt to kill her husband and his new lover. She also murders her psychologist after he assaults her, before going to her own death, which sees her killed by a panther at the zoo.

The reason for the harness is that the cat won't go outside. I don't blame her: so far, her experiences outside have involved being taken from her mother, and being taken to the vet. She has never liked unpredictability – loud noises, sudden movements, being picked up – and was so affected by her operation that I have left introducing her to the outside world rather late. *We'll do it in spring,* I said to myself. But now that spring is appearing, it isn't quite going as planned.

We bought the harness because I thought it might stop Mackerel from running off in a panic and being hit by a car. The thing is, every time we are able to get a hold of her for long enough to put the harness on her, she simply plays dead. She lies on her stomach like a statue and refuses to move.

Sometimes I see myself from the outside: a childless, thirty-something freelancer with a cat on a lead that won't cooperate, and I can't help but note that this is not how I pictured my life turning out. I think about the girls at home who had children young, and how I used to pity them, when actually now they'd probably pity me. I think about how I used to comfort myself with the fact that at least I still had my figure, but these days wherever I look, I see women with children who are slimmer than I. These are not pleasant thoughts, but womanhood can sometimes feel like a ruthless race – against our peers, and sometimes against the timelines of our own mothers (mine was thirty) – and we are forced to rely on schadenfreude for comfort: *At least, at least, at least. Well, at least I have my baby,* I imagine women who are mothers thinking. In a patriarchy, a baby trumps everything.

Well, at least I have the cat, I think. Even if she is an oddball. Who cares? I'm an oddball, too.

After I found Aurelie and family, my time in Paris became one of the happiest periods of my life. I think the feeling of loving domestic chaos reminded me of my own home, and though the children were not always easy, I would make difficult moments into a game. To get the five-year-old in the shower, for example, we would pretend he was a penguin. He'd waddle in and flap his arms while I hosed him down.

Outside of childcare, my time was my own. I found a job waitressing in a crêperie via a man I met in a bar, and the hours – a split shift covering lunch and dinner – were perfect, because I would pick up the children during the gap. I started writing for an English-language magazine (my first article was an exposé of the mistreatment of au pairs) and spent Sundays at the Shakespeare and Company writers' group, followed by a trip to the brasserie next door. I made friends with poets and authors, went out dancing.

I grew thin. I lived off cigarettes, coffee, tinned tabbouleh and crêpes.

I had delusions of glamour. I took up smoking and would sit on my windowsill in a kimono, listening to the sound of the opera singer who lived opposite practising her arias as the sun sank behind the rooftops. I didn't have a view of the Eiffel Tower here, but it somehow felt more Parisian in the heart of the Left Bank, a stone's throw from the cafés all the writers I had read about frequented. I wrote prolifically during this time, mostly about men, none of it very good. Nevertheless, I began to believe that I could do it, and that with practice, I could get better.

Men seemed to kiss me wherever I went.

One man kissed me on the steps of the Sorbonne as we waited for the first Metro, the end of the joint we had shared crushed, still-warm, on the marble.

Another man, an artist, kissed me in the darkness of a Liars gig, then took me home to his room, empty of everything except sculptures made from plastic cutlery.

Another man kissed me in a snowstorm on the Boulevard

Saint-Germain, then again, and again, and again, everywhere, for a week, until he flew to Stockholm. Tucked inside a book within the square of a black-and-white photobooth picture, he is kissing me still, his hands in my hair.

Another man kissed me under the weeping willow tree at the tip of the Île de la Cité. He was tall and dark and had a large scar down one side of his face. This was the man I chose.

Just over a decade after my year of Parisian freedom came my year of self-imprisonment – 2016, the year after the terorist attacks. Agoraphobia is particularly difficult to cure, because the more you avoid places, the more you start to associate them with danger.

In this way, I understand the cat's mentality. Why go outside when the indoors feels so safe? I believe that she was always a nervous kitten. I could see it in that first ever video. Nevertheless, if life events – her mother abandoning her, an early injury, medical complications, two locked-down humans who lavished her with attention – had been different, she may not have been so frightened of the outside. Another writer, the novelist Eli Goldstone, adopted two of Mackerel's sisters, Porridge and Pudding, and the similarities are uncanny. I see their expressions and their mannerisms, and it is unmistakable. Except *they* love to go outside (she says, however, that they love even more to come back in).

My social life suffered the year that I was agoraphobic, but not as much as it could have. I had learned from my single mother how to make fun in the domestic sphere. She was largely housebound because of my brother's needs, and many of her coupled-up friends stopped inviting her to dinner parties. There's a cartoon by the Finnish cartoonist Anna Härmälä which, spoofing a medieval manuscript, tells the story of the banishment of the 'single mother witch' from the 'village of couples'. 'Be gone, witch!' the women shout. 'She will steal our men and remind us that relationships are fragile and can end!'

My mother dealt with this by blasting Led Zeppelin, drinking wine, and entertaining her other single-mother friends at home.

The year I couldn't leave the house was the year my husband razed the overgrown patch of brambles to the rear of the building and built me a garden, so I entertained there or in the kitchen. My friends, to their eternal credit, made the effort to come and see me, especially my best friend (who was single at the time, and who I have never avoided because of the suspicion that she might steal my husband). It was my mother who taught me that, even with caring responsibilities, the domestic sphere needn't be a prison.

'There's a whole world out there!' I say to the cat, as she shrinks away from the open front door. Outside, the bulbs are coming up and there are buds on the cherry tree. 'You could be out there chasing butterflies!'

She is impassive.

I won't rush her. She'll get there in her own time.

When I was having therapy, I would sometimes talk to my mother about things that had happened during my childhood and, though I tried not to frame these in an accusatory manner, she would become defensive or apologetic, as though any unhappy moment in my early life could be traced back to her, a failing. Once, I threw a glass at the wall, not from rage at her, but from rage at my father, who was not even present.

I have a good relationship with my father, but I believe that in order to have fulfilling relationships with our parents in adulthood, we need to come to terms with the fact that they are human, that they make mistakes, and that – if they were part of a heterosexual pairing – they are operating within a structure that is unfair to both of them, but especially unfair to the woman, who bears the burden of care.

Many of my female friends have felt anger towards their fathers (many of my male friends, too, actually), and much of that anger is to do with either absence or betrayal, which is in itself a kind of absence. A father has the privilege to absent himself from the structures that he finds oppressive in a way that most women do not.

And yet not one of them has ever expressed their anger towards their fathers, just as I did not throw the glass against the wall of my father's house, but against the wall of my mother's. At the root of this seems to be the belief that our fathers are vulnerable, that to reveal these feelings to them would hurt them too deeply, or that they lack the emotional tools to properly manage their offspring's fury. Unlike our mothers, who bear the brunt of our distress, as they often always have.

In other words, we consider our mothers to be strong. Our mothers can take it.

Bad things happen to me and my family.

Part of the therapeutic process involved understanding that I had had a happy childhood. That it had not been easy, and that at times my brother's needs had dominated, and that there were, shall we say, events (a fire, two floods, divorce, seizures). And those events probably contributed to my developing post-traumatic stress, my inner belief that disaster was coming for me. But I came to understand that these things had not broken me. I had been surrounded by love, which I had never doubted. This is the most important thing that you can give a child, and I had it. It was a privilege. The greatest.

It is only by looking back on my treatment that I realise what has been going on these past few years: on the one hand, I believe that I am too broken to have a child, that I cannot give her what she deserves.

On the other, I know that the love I have to give would be gigantic.

I look at the photo of my brother on my bedside table: his gentle smile, his big hand blurred as he runs it over Rosa's fur. I have held up well, but it has been fifteen months, now, since I have seen his big grin greeting me in person.

I write to my brother's GP, asking again what they have been doing with their spare doses of vaccine and if it would be possible for him to have one. My aunt, a doctor, helps me write the email.

Two days later, they phone the care home to say he is on the list. Joy!

The crocuses are coming up when Shakes tells me that she is pregnant. Her cat has been all over her, she says. It's the pregnancy hormones. She has wanted this fiercely. The words on my screen blur as I feel the usual mix of delight and jealousy. It feels as though everyone in my life is either pregnant or a new parent. She is the second to announce this month, my old friend, and I am full of happiness for her, mixed with sadness at my longing for the same. 'It's just cells multiplying right now,' she says, with the typical rationality of a medic, and for a moment I feel annoyed at her words, even though I know I'd be similar. It's the superstitious Irish in us both.

I walk across the city to meet my friend and her twin

boys – my godson and his brother – in the park. The day is blustery, but after a long, cold winter it is just about warm enough to be outside. When I see my godson and his brother, I am in awe of their rapid growth and development. For months I have been painting and varnishing a small chair from my own childhood for them, agonising over the split, warped wood in one corner and worrying about splinters. It occurs to me that now they are too big for it.

They are talking and singing. As I often do in these moments, I think of my brother, whose words were lost, or never came, and reflect on how, in hindsight, it was obvious that he wasn't neurotypical. I remember writing in my school book, age ten, that 'Mum and Dad think my brother is autistic', and my mother saying, gently: 'Darling, he *is* autistic.' For a long time, I assumed my younger self was in denial, but now I think that, in practice, it simply didn't matter all that much to me. He was still my smiling, blue-eyed little brother; any medical label was secondary.

'Let's look at the crocuses,' I say to my godson. I tiptoe through them, careful not to crush their blooms, expecting him to do the same. But he is clumsy and ungainly, as toddlers are, and bulldozes through them. 'Never mind,' I say, 'let's look from over here.'

My friend and her family are leaving the city, a move about which she has mixed feelings. I watch the speed with which her boys charge about, and ask her how she manages not to collapse from fear every time she takes them out. It's not that I am against raising children in the city, but with a history of trauma – a condition my friend also shares – I wonder how it is doable without suffering from extreme hypervigilance and constant panic. She confesses that she is rarely at ease, and that she has had scary experiences when out and about with them. Once, a strange man tried to lure one of the twins away. I tell her that it sounds as though she is doing the right thing by opting for a quieter life.

It is hard to wave them off. I formed a friendship with this woman, who is married to my cousin, years ago, but it was during her pregnancy that it became profound. After a traumatic birth that almost killed her and her babies, and which in the aftermath awakened some disturbing events from her past, she became fearful of the outside world. I tried to visit every week, determined not to drop off as child-free friends can sometimes do, conscious that – thousands of miles from her family and wrestling with post-traumatic stress – she might need someone. Now, like so many of my peers, she was leaving, and I knew that I would miss her desperately.

On the walk home, I think: *Maybe I can do this. Maybe I can be a mother.* And though I love the city, perhaps, for the sake of my sanity, it will need to be somewhere else.

When I was at my most mentally unwell, I used to tell my husband that I wanted to leave the city. I want a cottage in the countryside, I would say, with a rose garden. I am sick of being frightened here, forgetting, naturally, that the rural can be just as menacing, and holds its own horrors.

My husband, who is older than I and fell out of love with the city long before, could have taken advantage of this, but he didn't. He knew it was my trauma talking, that to make decisions based on fear would not serve me in the long run. And so we stayed.

'We meet our unconscious in our own destinies.' I have tried, to no avail, to find the terrible therapist's quote in the writings of Carl Jung. It has rung in my head ever since he said it, and over the years, from time to time, I would come back to it as though worrying at a longstanding scab. It is only recently that I have come, I think, to understand it. I suspect what he was referring to was this: 'The psychological rule says that when an inner situation is not made conscious, it happens outside, as fate.'

What I think he meant is that until I reconciled my fear of death, I would continue to believe that terrible things were destined to happen to me. But then the sentence that follows complicates things:

That is to say, when the individual remains undivided and does not become conscious of his inner opposite, the world must perforce act out the conflict and be torn into opposing halves.

248

This is where I couldn't help but feel that I was being blamed, that my inability to solve my inner fears led to them somehow mystically manifesting in the real world, as though I were attracting the male violence, or was in a state of perpetual victimhood. This, I could not allow. To me, the violence wrought against me was extraneous and undeserved; this was non-negotiable.

To choose not to be a mother would be, for me, a decision based on fear. There are many rational, logical, intellectual reasons not to have children, but none of them are as relevant to me as the false belief that continues to dominate: that catastrophe will inevitably befall me, as though I am somehow cursed to be an unfit mother.

Again, I am letting my trauma do the talking. I resolve not to, but it is hard.

And yet. I have kept the cat alive for almost a year. I have fed her and cared for her, and yes, fretted about her, but the worry is diminishing as I become more confident and she becomes bigger and less squashable. There are things that I would have done differently, of course, were I to do it again, but overall, I think I've made a success of it.

In Paris, I had no fear. I finished work around 1am and walked up the Boulevard Saint-Germain and down the Rue de Sèvres, or sometimes took a detour through the darkened streets around Saint-Sulpice. I don't remember ever feeling afraid. I mostly looked in the shop windows, fantasising about being the sort of woman who could stroll into Sonia Rykiel or Isabel Marant and buy an outfit. I never hurried. I liked the silence of the cityscape, empty of tourists.

I hardly ever saw another being, except for the cats. Walking past the decrepit, boarded-up Hôtel Lutetia, which had housed the Gestapo during the war, I would shiver at its haunted feel of faded grandeur. Years later, on my first trip back to Paris after the attacks, when the Lutetia had been renovated and transformed into a five-star luxury hotel, I would stay there in a suite (you could also say that, after my year of dilapidation, I too had been renovated). I was supposed to be writing an article that saw me following in the footsteps of the city's women writers, though when I pointed out that Jean Rhys's alcoholism drew her generally towards depressing dive bars, the luxury travel magazine decided it would be preferable to channel Colette, and sent me to a restaurant where every course, even dessert, contained truffles.

I was living in a future that I could never have predicted for myself.

While staying at the Hôtel Lutetia, I would stand, champagne-buzzed in silk pyjamas, on the balcony, looking down at the street below and imagining the teenage waitress who had sauntered past it countless times on her midnight walks looking up at me. She would think me lucky. She was entirely unaware of the freedom she'd been blessed with. Such nonchalance, such insouciance. Such an absence of fear wouldn't be allowed to stand.

On a dark suburban street, three men stopped us and said something in French to my boyfriend that I did not understand, though at this point I was almost fluent. It was only later, when we were safely indoors, that he told me what they had said, though he tried to keep it from me.

'Tu veut la faire tournée?'

Do you want to pass her around?

A young woman has been murdered, and the women of the city are in mourning and in rage. She was just walking home, we keep saying, as we all have, as we all should be free to, without fear. I feel the old fury returning, the fury which, after my attack, was the only thing that allowed me momentum. I could curl up into a ball, or I could choose to be powered by anger. I chose the latter.

My feminism, when I found it, was underpinned by rage. It was unpalatable, this rage, but it also kept me alive. I wanted to smash up the world and rebuild it, piece by piece, into a place of safety and warmth for women.

I wanted to hurt the men who did this to me, to us. I wanted them to pay.

But I could not live inside this rage forever and not become consumed by it. Just as I now fear the self-abnegation of motherhood, I came to fear then the obliterating power of my anger. In time, I learned how to channel it productively into writing and activism.

Still, every now and again, it stirs.

The world feels colder than it has ever felt, at this time. It is a now over a year since the sickness started, but the spring is not as we had hoped. It is freezing and sodden. Yet the women come out to lay flowers for their sister and are manhandled by policemen for their trouble. It was a policeman who murdered her. The show of defiance – we are still supposed to stay indoors and not gather – and solidarity threatens them, these frightened little men.

Perhaps it is this, in the end, that will break me. I do not think I have any tears left. But they flow.

What was your daughter doing out so late?

It is no wonder that women traditionally kept cats. Unlike a dog, a cat does not require walking, and does not need an escort in the unsafe streets at night. A cat can come and go with a freedom that a woman, confined to the home, historically never had. It is only when a woman – a witch

– took a cat's shape that she could prowl the city undetected and unmolested.

'Everybody, everybody, everybody wants to be a cat.'

My brother played the tape about the Parisian cats over, and over, and over.

Don't talk to any strange men, my mother used to say to me, before I left the house. My whole childhood, I heard this warning. From a very young age, I knew there were men who would try to hurt me, that I was to resist if I could. You scream and you kick and you fight, she said, showing me how to knee them in the balls, or put my fingers in their eyes. You fight like a cat, dirtily and noisily. And this is what I did. This is how I survived. My mother saved my life.

Why bring a daughter into this world, only to have to teach her to fight like a cat?

I think of a witch, taking the form of a vampire cat. I imagine her prowling the city at night, tearing the guts from these men.

Contemplating the disrupted vigil, I think of the suffragettes, how the police beat and brutalised them, ripping open their blouses to grope their breasts, and pulling up their skirts. Over 100 years later, a photograph of a red-headed young woman protestor being held to the ground by male officers renders me livid. In another photograph, a young woman is led away wearing a T-shirt bearing a Jenny Holzer quote: 'ABUSE OF POWER COMES AS NO SURPRISE'.

I wanted to be with them, but I did not go. I was afraid of how I'd get home afterwards in the dark. Instead, I lit a candle for her and put it in the window.

I've been thinking a lot about bravery. The judge commended me for mine, though I do not believe that I was any braver that night than any other woman: it was merely a case of fight or flight, and my primitive brain chose fight. It is true that my mother taught me the skills – though she had never told me to give chase, which is what I did, recklessly and stupidly. But I could equally have frozen, as many women do. Trauma has taught me that we have little control over our animal brains, and yet we feel shame because of their reactions, whatever those are.

Women who choose not to have children are brave, I think. They face the judgement of society. They take the risk that one day they may regret their choice, which is something that people say to them – 'You'll change your mind' – as though having a child to future-proof against regret is enough of a reason to reproduce. My friends who say they don't want children are adamant that they will not change their minds, and I believe them, though I also find myself hoping that the longing won't come for them, because the longing seems to know no logic. It has a power of its own.

The burning of the planet means that we are seeing an increase in anti-natalist arguments. Population is the problem, these advocates, who always seem to be men, cry. As ever, the blame lies with women, and their unruly bodies.

Silvia Federici puts the witch hunts within the context of demographic collapse. We are seeing a similar panic now, as politicians and thinktanks start to worry about the 'baby bust'. Will women again be put at the service of population increase? We are seeing movements against birth control and abortion on a global scale.

On the other hand, women are speaking out about their refusal to reproduce. How long until the world turns on them?

My colleague writes of how, were she to have a child, by the time her child is ten, a quarter of the world's insects will be gone.

I myself worry about the insects. I remember being small, butterfly spotting, and how I spent most of last summer in the garden and saw hardly any. In summers past, a window left open at night meant a room swarming with insects; now there is nothing. Like a windscreen after a long drive: empty.

'The biggest contribution any individual living in affluent nations can make is to not have children,' she continues. She also writes that, sometimes, she feels the longing for a daughter, for the weight of her in her arms, with 'staggering intensity'.

I admire her so much.

Mackerel still refuses to go outside. Instead, she sits in front of the television and hunts the bees on *Gardeners' World*.

I don't remember it being a chore to care for six children, including, sometimes, a baby. I loved each of those exuberant children, and when the end of my time with them came, I did not want to leave. I wanted to stay in Paris, waitressing and writing. Instead, I signed the student loan papers and packed up my flea market wardrobe and left.

In the years since I left Paris, I have seen the children

at intervals and watched them transform, one by one, into adults.

Not long after I first got together with my husband, I took a trip to Paris alone, and stayed in the family's apartment. It was summer, and most of them were in the south, but the eldest son would come and go, and I was astonished to see that he was no longer twelve. It was like some sort of magic trick.

I had changed, too, of course: though not yet in my mid-twenties, I had transitioned from 'Mademoiselle' to 'Madame' in restaurants. Men no longer stopped me to tell me that I was '*charmante*', nor followed me with their eyes on the Metro. Though I confess that I missed feeling beautiful, the overwhelming feeling was one of liberation.

My previous two visits to the city had, unfortunately, been defined by my ex. It took years to wriggle free from his emotional hook. Each time I visited the city, I seemed to conjure him like a phantom, and afterwards I would wake up in his bed, cursing myself.

The last time I went to him was the year before my attack. I was living in Italy and was desperately homesick, so, under the influence of heavy painkillers, I booked the flight. To flee to Paris seemed less of a personal failure than to run away home.

It had been a mistake. I left his squalid apartment and went to Shakespeare and Company, where I begged Sylvia for a bed. She did not have one available and, quite rightly, seemed to have little patience for aspiring writers seeking refuge from romantic turmoil. I went to the Gare du Nord and took the train north to my aunt's. 'I've been expecting you,' she said, when I arrived, having been tipped off by my mother as to my quixotic plans. She too had also once had to flee a Frenchman in a hurry.

This trip, however, was entirely my own. I ate and drank alone in restaurants and on terraces, unmolested, relishing the August emptiness and heat. I returned to the Jardins Babylone and Luxembourg and lay on the grass, reading. I browsed the windows of the boutiques as I had as a teenage waitress, and, though I was marginally less poor, having started writing for newspapers, bought nothing. I went to galleries and sat in front of paintings and sculptures for hours. I wrote.

I did not go out at night.

There will have been a moment when she knew that she was going to die, and it is this that I cannot stop thinking about. When the man's hands closed around my neck, my body rushed towards that moment and was pulled back. I was lucky.

My husband tells me that I need to detach myself from this case. Perhaps he can sense the old madness returning; I know I can. When I sleep, the nightmares have returned.

Goya was also plagued by nightmares. In his engraving

The Sleep of Reason Produces Monsters, he personifies these frightening dreams with all kinds of devilish creatures, including a black cat that lurks menacingly behind the artist's sleeping back, its eyes fixed on the viewer. When I look at this image, it is as though I feel it: the infernal onslaught that the dreamer is subject to. I have felt it. The nightmares I suffered after both attacks were worse than any horror film I have ever seen, featuring Nazis and torture and hangings and mutilation. Guns were held to my temple for what seemed like hours; my loved ones were killed or taken from me. I would wake sobbing, in despair.

The nightmares are never a good sign.

I find myself thinking not only of this young woman, but of all of them, and of my friends who have been raped, or assaulted, or locked indoors by men. I think of Lisa, and the sound of her boyfriend calling her a cunt radiating through the walls, and of my friend from school who was taken to live in a women's refuge when we were ten.

I think of my younger self, walking to the tube on my way out for the evening, red lipstick, of the respectable-looking businessman who muttered under his breath, 'Whore mouth,' and of the night my ex shook me so hard that my teeth rattled, and who phoned my mother, sobbing and apologising and babbling drunkenly and incoherently, after I locked myself in the toilet. She thought he had killed me, then.

I think of my senior male colleague, who shoved his tongue down my throat when I was too full of alcohol to move; of how, helped by a female colleague, I was able to get home, where I lay on the bathroom floor, immobile, thankful I was not lying somewhere else. I think of how being in that building felt afterwards, knowing I could see him at any moment; of how my stomach would physically lurch with disgust at the thought.

And I think, inevitably, of being strangled, and thinking I would die on that pavement, and wanting more than ever to live.

I cannot stop thinking about her and wishing that the world could be different.

The cat seems to know when I am on edge. She follows me around the house, and curls up next to me in bed. I remember how frightened she was after her operation, and how I slept with her on the kitchen floor. Her presence now feels almost as though she is returning the favour. She is being a good friend to me at a time when I am separated from the people in my life.

I wonder how many of the world's 'crazy cat ladies' have been victims of male violence. Do they identify with the stray, wounded animals they take in, the ill-treated creatures that live on the margins? Or is it that they have lost their faith in humans? In comparison to men, a cat asks very little of you. They are easy to love.

~

Not far from my house is an infamous women's prison, now closed. Jean Rhys was sent there, charged with assaulting a neighbour after his dog attacked her cats.

Next to it is a newly built library, named The Cat and Mouse Library. It's a name that appears cosy and child-friendly, when in fact it has distinctly unpleasant roots, commemorating as it does the 1913 Prisoners (Temporary Discharge for Ill-Health) Act, commonly known as the Cat and Mouse Act. This act of parliament was drawn up in response to public outrage regarding the force-feeding of hunger strikers at the prison. It enabled the temporary release of prisoners who were weakened by self-starvation, only for them to be rearrested and imprisoned later, when they had regained their health. The main victims of this act were campaigners for the women's suffrage movement.

I have a postcard that once belonged to my father, a reproduction of a poster campaigning against the Liberal government for their instigation of this act. It shows a suffragette, limp and pale in the jaws of a cat. Prey.

The act was intended to demoralise, but instead, on release, many of the activists bolted. The suffragettes established an all-female bodyguard unit nicknamed 'the Amazons', which protected released women from re-arrest using a variety of tactics – including hand-to-hand combat with the police. They learned jujitsu, and their particular brand of self-defence was nicknamed 'suffrajitsu'.

The name of the library was chosen to commemorate these women, and it contains a permanent exhibition honouring the suffragettes. The opening day's festivities included poetry performances, yoga and a baby jazz session.

There is safety and cosiness in my constricted domestic environment, as well as loneliness. Sometimes, living with my mother and my brother, it could feel as though we were shipwrecked. But our little trio (not counting the cats) made for a happy house that I still miss to this day. I sometimes wonder if more adults mourn their child-hoods than really let on, or if, because of the unique circumstances in which I was raised, a part of me will always be stuck there. I still find it sad that I do not live with my brother.

Though we made a tight unit, we were lucky to live in a community. Women friends drank wine or read plays with my mother; male friends fixed the toilet or helped with odd jobs. Care workers took my brother for walks off the books; young friends of mine babysat (one of these friends has since become a foster parent, and says she was inspired to do so by my brother).

It is this social fabric that has been missing from my life – since the pandemic, certainly, but even before that, as friends began to leave the city. It is only this year that I have truly realised, or perhaps accepted, that your existence is nothing without the friendship, love and solidarity offered by other people.

You can find a family whether you have children or not.

Aurelie's second-eldest daughter has adopted a cat, a stray tabby from their house in the south. She is named Aya, and she lives in Paris now.

It was Aurelie who offered us refuge on the night of the attacks, who opened the door when we woke them, late, by banging on their windows. It was the only place that I could think of going.

I have been enriched by my work for and friendship with this family. I have watched the three-year-old become a dancer, seen her pirouette at the Royal Ballet School. I have dropped off the baby at the train station, old enough now to travel alone across France. On one visit, when he was smaller, Aurelie told me of how she carried him across the road to the children's hospital in her arms after a seizure, and I have always held this image of motherhood in my mind, almost like a religious icon.

I have never been a follower of Mary – but a Guinness-loving Parisian mother-of-six who told me that she once, while pregnant, ate seventy oysters at an all-you-can-eat seafood festival? I can get behind her.

There are images of my own mother, too, which glow like icons in my mind.

My mother making me a cardboard carousel.

My mother at Halloween, dressed as a fortune-teller, tricking us into drawing eyebrows and moustaches on our faces with blackened cork as part of an old parlour game.

My mother dancing in the kitchen with my brother.

My mother at the shore of the lake, watching him toss in stones to make ripples.

My mother letting me, at twelve, rest my head on her breasts as I cried about being flat-chested and saying: 'Wait until you get pregnant.'

My mother walking into the room wearing the outfit devised for her by teachers at my brother's special needs school during art class, attributed, like all these projects, to his hand. The poncho. The newspaper hat.

My mother, her friend, and I using my brother's spinning art kit to make food paintings, dribbling Worcestershire sauce, ketchup, mustard and wine on to the rotating squares of cardboard, laughing.

My mother, returning from a New Year's Eve party, handing my friend a torch so that he could find the weed he had lost down the back of the sofa, then putting me to bed, with a bucket.

Some of these pictures are sad.

My mother crying in the car because the social worker

has said: 'There is no point teaching him to speak, because he'd just talk rubbish, anyway.'

My mother walking me back to the street where I was attacked, because I insisted I'd be able to return there, and gently helping me into the car when it became very obvious that I would not.

My mother's rage during the divorce.

My mother has been alone throughout this pandemic, and once she phoned me in tears and said she felt like a failure because she hadn't had much 'career' success in her life.

She is wrong. She could never be a failure. Even those sadder images are magnificent. My mother is magnificent.

Though it is technically spring, the grey cold feels interminable, and I can feel myself getting very low. Throughout this, my husband and that cat have helped protect me from depression, as has writing this, whatever this is. Now things are starting to feel hopeless, and my efforts to find small pockets of joy in my days are becoming more strained. You can only fight against a riptide for so long, before your limbs get heavy and you start to sink.

Missing people does not help. It has been eighteen months since I saw my brother in person, and though our movements are restricted, I am wondering how much longer I can take.

I read an article that cites a study saying that only ten per cent of women without children decided on that path voluntarily. It links to a post called '50 ways not to be a mother', which lists some of the reasons for involuntary childlessness, as cited by women campaigning for greater compassion and understanding of their status.

1) Being single and unable to find a suitable relationship from your mid-thirties onwards.
9) Being with a partner who says they want children later . . . but the time is never right for them.
16) Miscarriage.
32) Caring for a sick, elderly, disabled or vulnerable family member during our fertile years.
49) Chemotherapy.

The grief that some of these women feel is monumental, but it isn't talked about. Their pain does not always subside, as I confess I assumed it might one day (and it was this belief that made the thought of not having a child myself more manageable). Why is there such a stigma to wanting, but not getting? Why is their thwarted longing so tinged with shame?

I have felt it myself, a desire to underplay how much I want this. How my need feels bodily, visceral. How its power leaves me frightened, but also in awe.

Longing isn't fashionable, I suppose. In a capitalist economy, we are led to believe that we can buy our way out of our unfulfilled desires, that there is always a product designed to fill the void. This is not so with motherhood. If you are rich, money can certainly change hands. But for the vast majority, whether you become a mother is not something that can be controlled or even understood. Despite huge advances in medical science, the material world doesn't always have a solution.

It is the mystery of conception that leads so many women to turn to magical thinking. It feels as though, in almost everything I read about thwarted reproductive desire, the woman writing eventually turns to psychics or coins or cards or spells, or lighting candles in churches and temples, or praying, or ritual or herbal medicine. This may seem desperate to some, but to me it makes sense, this tempting of fate. So much of reproduction remains shrouded in mystery. Often, they can never tell a woman exactly why her womb lies empty (in the past, a witch might well have been blamed). And so some will try to bargain with destiny.

I'm reading the cards a lot at the moment, as I do when I feel lost. My mother always taught me to think of the question when I'm shuffling, and fanning them out with my left hand (more connected to the psychic side of your body, apparently, and though I do not believe this, I do it anyway). And as I do this, I constantly catch myself thinking:

Baby, baby, baby, baby, baby, baby.

I think I have found the answer to that silent question asked of women in their thirties: *What is your purpose?*

My answer is, to write. The sense of purpose that writing gives me is also what helps me live. The challenge of conveying to others the knotty contradictions I feel around motherhood, the mad desire undercut by all the fear, has kept me going. It's like a game, trying to pin down these swirling thoughts. I intend to keep playing it, even in the midst of intense sadness.

I suppose I now admit that this is indeed a book. I plough on, despite all my reservations about how admitting to this unfashionable longing makes me vulnerable, how it exposes my husband to speculations about our personal life, how other women might read it and think, *That's not how it is*, and become angry with me. Most of all, I worry that one day my child, if I have one, will read it and think, *She didn't want me.* Perhaps she will come home from the playground and, as I am undoing her duffle coat, she will say that another child told her that I had written a book all about not being sure if I wanted children.

I find myself rehearsing what I will say to her:

'Mama always wanted you; she was just scared. She spent so much of her life being afraid in those days.'

This would be true, though a simplified telling.

But then, people are so simplistic about these things. In my online reading, I keep coming across the admonishment that you should never have a child unless you are 100 per cent sure that you want to be a parent. Who are these people, blessed with so much certainty?

I have never been fully sure about anything. That is not how the anxious mind works. I twist decisions around and turn them over. I read, consult, converse, until the subject is exhausted. It is laborious, certainly, but I could never be accused of being thoughtless or impulsive. And, once I have decided, I generally feel at peace with my choice.

Perhaps to do this – to have a child – is what bravery means, for me. That is not the same as saying that to become a mother is the braver choice in all cases. But in writing this down, I have learned to recognise the things that frighten me because they are threats to my wellbeing, and those that frighten me but which I desperately want. That's what anxiety is: longing to do things your animal brain is convinced will destroy you. These things won't necessarily kill me, even if they feel, in the moment, terrifying. Like taking a taxi because you're convinced you'll be shot on the bus, avoidance always seems like the easier path, but it isn't – not for me.

As much as I respect my reservations when I observe them in other women, when I note them in myself I have started to understand what I am trying to do. I am trying to rationalise my unfulfilled longing. I am trying to come up with reasons for why I am not yet a mother. My mind is trying to understand a bodily desperation that feels, at times, beyond language.

Adrienne Rich writes that: 'only the willingness to share private and sometimes painful experience can enable women to create a collective description of the world that can be truly ours'.

Our understanding of the collective is different from that of the second-wave feminists, but nonetheless the experience that many of us share is that of violence wrought against our bodies and our minds by men. In this sense, we are a community.

My experience can only be my own. My longing to be a mother, and my feeling at times of being at war with that longing, cannot resonate with every woman. Yet I cannot help but feel that there must be others out there like me, who, in the aftermath of trauma, fear motherhood – an institution created by men. We fear its codes and its dialects, its strange, false-sounding cadences, its potential to make us strangers from ourselves.

Yet despite all the persuasive reasons against, we want

to find a way to embody it. We must find a new way of writing it.

I read an essay by Sigrid Nunez in which she writes of how hard it is to name a major novel by a canonical writer, male or female, that takes motherhood for its main subject, despite the fact that it is such a widely shared human experience.

For a long time, she was right – she had written this before Ferrante, who said in an interview that 'motherhood seems to me one of those experiences which are ours alone and whose literary truth has yet to be explored'. I try to think of examples. *Beloved*, I think, perhaps, or *The Handmaid's Tale*.

It's true, though, that there aren't enough (more are being written every year, and some will doubtless join the canon). There are fewer still that, like Sheila Heti's *Motherhood*, contemplate whether to embark on it at all. That whole novel is framed as a question, and it is a question that Heti takes seriously and intellectually, as an artist, and as a thinker. The decision about whether or not to make and grow a human in one's body and raise her in the world, and what that means, is surely one of the most fundamental philosophical questions that exists. Yet this state of not-motherhood or almost-motherhood is often a silent one.

Even the most famous mother of all has no say in her state: she is simply informed of the matter by a messenger from the patriarch.

Even before motherhood was a choice for women, who, before the advent of contraception, had little say in when their pregnancies occurred, they will have pondered what it meant to birth and raise a human, and how that affected their identities. These thoughts, dismissed as silly and domestic, have been largely unrecorded by history, are deemed unworthy of literature. They are footnotes, trivialities.

As though the home and the woman within it hasn't been the backdrop to the consciousness of every person who has ever lived. As though it doesn't shape all of us, and the ideas we have about the world and other people, resonating throughout our lives, manifesting in all that we do.

We have given up on the harness. Still, the cat sits on the doorstep, gazing out impassively at our sunny street, refusing to go further.

It is funny how I have shifted from being secretly pleased that Mackerel does not want to go outside, because it saves me the worry, to wishing she would and wanting her to taste freedom. Perhaps it is that I am recognising, as a result of my own sadness, the fact that no one should stay at home for this long a time without social contact. It is not natural. It makes people crazy. It is making me crazy.

In late March, I crack, and take the train north to see my brother. First, I take a test. The line reads negative, and I am struck by how much it resembles a pregnancy test.

How many of those have I taken in my life? The result has always been the same and always, always, met with relief.

Though government restrictions are still in place, there is an exception for vulnerable people and, having waited long enough for his vaccine immunity to kick in, I now pose far less of a risk to my brother, infection-wise.

The train is eerie in its quietness, and as I watch the scenery – flat, green fields and blue spring sky – flash past, I can feel myself becoming pre-emptively emotional. Usually, I save the tears for the way home, but it has been so long now that the thought of being with him again feels momentous and somehow historical, even though we are just two people in a world of billions, many of whom have also been kept apart.

To stop myself from crying I think of some of the memories of my brother that make me smile, and have sustained me through our separation:

My cherubic baby brother, at four or five, having just flooded the house after leaving the bath to run, looking up at my father, who was naked apart from a dressing gown and baling frantically, and saying: 'Want to go swimming.'

My brother swimming in the cold, clear mountain river on a hot day.

My brother jumping into a fountain to try and escape me chasing him, and it being far deeper than he'd anticipated, and him going right under.

My brother laughing because I put Radox in the jacuzzi at the posh spa. How the bubbles reached the ceiling.

My brother blowing bubbles on his birthday. Him blowing out his candles for the first time (we didn't think he could). Him dancing on his own in the living room, my mother and I in the doorway, watching, then joining him. All the times we danced after that. Singing him to sleep. The way, when he was small, he would sometimes get into bed with me, this little boy who disliked being hugged or touched, and would curl up and go to sleep and I would know: *He loves me.* My brother laughing and saying, 'Bloody cat, bloody cat, bloody cat.'

When I get off the train, I am gifted a new memory: a smile big enough to split his face, a walk together with my mother along the canal, the sun bright and the air crisp. I watch him snaffling the brownies she has brought for him, and I am struck, as I always am, by the fact that he is a man now, and how much time has passed.

I vow not to squander any more, but of course I will. We always do. The time we have with the people we love never feels like enough.

Three hours later, I take the train home, and cry, but this time not from sadness. It has been one of the defining experiences of my life, loving him, despite all the fear that has come with it.

On my walk, I see another 'Lost Cat' poster. Poor Morpheus! I hope he comes home.

'Do you think that [brother's name] understands about death?' I asked my mother, once. I was in the middle of therapy at the time, and was finally articulating fears that I had never found the words for before. One was that my parents would die and that my brother wouldn't understand where they had gone, and would think they had stopped coming to see him.

It was a thought so sad that I could barely express it.

'Does anyone?' my mother replied.

The magnolia are blossoming, and on our evening walks, the air fills with the scent. 'It's so beautiful out there,' I tell Mackerel. 'You'd love it. Really.' Worried about her lack of outside stimulation, I buy her a rotating, fluttering butterfly toy. The idea is that she will hunt it, but instead she just stands next to it and allows its wings to massage her face. I'm not sure how long she would survive in the wild.

It's my husband's birthday: a warm, sunny spring day. His brother and his partner and their daughter come, and we all sit in the garden. I make a quiche of asparagus and goat's cheese, and serve it with new potatoes and watercress in a mustard dressing. We drink Crémant, and for afters we eat strawberries and cream. My niece, born shortly before the first lockdown and now just over a year old, screams throughout. She is not used to the company of strangers. This is something lockdown babies seem to share in common: not long ago, we bumped into a friend of my husband's, walking his baby daughter, who started wailing the moment we peered over the pram. 'She cries when she sees people without masks on,' he said.

My brother- and sister-in-law keep apologising, not that they have anything to apologise for. People who tut at crying children are arseholes. My brother, being autistic, tantrumed for far longer than a neurotypical child, so I have experienced the full spectrum of judgemental reactions from the general public. (Sometimes, people are nice, and it is those moments that save you. My mother recalls my brother having a screaming fit in the changing rooms at the local swimming pool. A young woman said to her friend: 'Look! Look at that little boy!' and my mother braced herself for judgement. Instead, she said: 'Oh, isn't he beautiful!')

So their daughter cries, and we don't care – we are just happy to see them. It has been so long. We have only met their daughter once or twice. I read this week that, in Japan, new parents are sending their relatives 'babies' filled with rice that match the birth weight of the real child and bear a picture of their face, to hug instead of the newborns.

After they leave, it is very quiet. We walk up the street

in companionable silence, and I feel for a moment almost giddy with freedom. 'So,' I say, eventually, 'has it made you want your own?'

We laugh, but the truth is, it has. It always does.

The following weekend, Ash and Ghazal come over to sit in the garden. My jovial husband keeps offering Ghazal a glass of champagne, despite her repeated refusals. 'You can get a taxi!' he keeps saying.

She is obviously pregnant, but I'm not sure how to signal to him to shut up without them seeing. Then she tells us, and we all raise our glasses. She is so happy.

When I go upstairs to get the food, I pick up Mackerel and hold her in my arms. I tap on the window and wave, and they look up, but our house is tall and they are many metres below. 'I wanted to show you the cat,' I tell them, when I return downstairs, but they hadn't been able to see. Later, I try explaining about what I am writing. 'It's about the cat,' I say, 'but it is also about not being sure if you should have a child.'

Later, when we are briefly alone together, I confess my longing to Ghazal. I have told many friends of my longing, but this time I do not qualify it with my list of reasons against.

After they leave, I feel pathetic.

The country is opening up again. It is a cold, sunny day, the perfect day for eating oysters and drinking wine at a pavement table, which is what B and I do. Then I have a rare steak with a crisp green salad, and a glass of red. It is so good to be with a friend again, laughing and eating food that we haven't had to cook ourselves.

B says that she wants to start trying for a baby as soon as she is married, this summer. L is pregnant with her second child, and H has a two-year-old. Soon, I could be the only one left, the cat who overslept, tricked into thinking she had time.

Time. I'm so tired of thinking about time.

After seeing my brother, I can feel the bad thoughts passing. I am not so angry; I am sleeping better. The news is still depressing, but I feel hope for the future. I have the impression that I have been pulled back from the edge of something.

My husband is going away, to be with his family for a week or so. I could go, too, but someone needs to be with the cat, and after a year in close quarters, I am craving some time alone. Before all this happened, I was a solitary person, spending many hours a day on my own, reading and writing. Since then, I have adapted – I used to be unable to write at all if there was someone else in the house – but the thought of being able to do whatever I want without having to consult anyone else for their preferences is very appealing.

I am also excited to let Mackerel sleep in my bed with me.

It's been many months since my husband has seen some of his siblings, and a few since he has seen his parents, so he knows that the visit might be a little strange. We talk about how the emotions he feels might not all be happy ones; how he might too feel grief at the time that he has missed with the people he loves; how socially, things might be clumsy and awkward, and how that is OK.

I spend my first evening alone preparing an elaborate pasta dish. Afterwards, I watch a terrible romantic comedy about sperm donation, and finish it irritated that I have allowed its formulaic sentimentality to move me. Mackerel undertakes her usual evening routine after eating, which consists of sitting watchfully in a dark room, still but alert. We will regroup at bedtime.

Late into the evening, my husband calls me from the stillness of his parents' spare bedroom. I imagine him lying there in the dark. His voice is quiet and sad. He tells me that his father's hair has grown wild and bouffant, that everyone has aged. He tells me about seeing his nephew, a pandemic baby whom he has only met once before.

'But the thing that made me the most sad,' says my husband with a crack in his voice, 'was seeing Scampie. He's so old, and he looks so poorly.'

Scampie – a handsome, long-haired tabby cat – was originally my husband's sister's cat. He had been given to her as a kitten by a boyfriend. He was nervous and probably a bit traumatised from the shared flat they had lived in, or at least my husband always thought so. My sister-in-law says that Scampie was so fearsome that the two resident adult cats left the premises almost immediately, never to return.

My sister-in-law eventually split up with that boyfriend and moved to New Zealand to be with her new one, so Scampie moved in with the family. It was here that he consolidated his reputation as a bruiser, his favourite hobby being chasing and attacking dogs of all sizes. 'Get your cat off my dog!' distressed owners used to shout.

Scampie was loyal, even once catching the bus to school with my husband's younger sister, who had to remove him at the bus driver's request. He used to spend a lot of time with my husband when he was a teenager, sleeping in the garden annexe that became his bedroom (there were nine children) while he hotboxed it with his friends.

My favourite story about Scampie involves him using his rough little cat tongue to lick the top off a quiche that had been left in the kitchen, only for my husband to consume the rest of it drunkenly on his return home.

When my husband moved home after university, a bit lost, as we all are in those listless, depressing months, he would go out to the pub after his tedious data-entry job finished. At closing time, he would walk home through the darkened streets of his town. At some point during the journey, he told me, Scampie would always join him, escorting him back to his parents' house safely.

That cat is twenty now, and in the decade I have known him, he has become thinner. Sometimes he requires hand-feeding. But no one is ready to let him go.

I pass a disruptive night with Mackerel, who is so excited at being allowed into the bedroom that she spends most of it purring and demanding cuddles. Just as I drop off to sleep, I am awoken by the sound of my water glass smashing to the floor. Fearing that the glass will cut her paws, I get the Henry vacuum cleaner out: the cat's arch-nemesis. She makes herself scarce, as she always does, and I eventually find her curled up in her squishy bed, which she has been avoiding for the six months since I bought it, despite it being sprayed with catnip.

On the Saturday, I go out for a late lunch with J, L and A. The sun is shining, and we are all jubilant with the fact that we were able to eat at a restaurant again. J keeps ordering bottle after bottle of Gavi di Gavi until we are exuberantly drunk. We repair to my garden with more alcohol, where we have the sorts of honest conversations that you can only have when you're extremely inebriated and have been in government-enforced isolation for months on end. 'I think I want to have a baby,' I tell J, and we raise our glasses to each other.

We are all social distancing, then we all get drunk and hug each other.

They leave around ten, legless, and I come upstairs and make dinner. Looking at my phone, I see that my husband has sent a photo of Scampie being held in his mother's arms, his eyes and nose downcast. 'He passed away peacefully this morning,' he writes.

He waited, I find myself thinking. *He waited until his friend came home.*

It hadn't quite been like that, my husband tells me on the phone later. Scampie had deteriorated overnight, but he hadn't died of natural causes. He had been taken to the vet. The vet had said that to take Scampie home and let him die slowly would be inhumane, and that it would be better to put him down. No one else could face doing it, so my husband said he would be with him. Bizarrely, the vet asked him to select an urn for Scampie's ashes before they went through to end his life.

I manage to hold it together for most of the call, but the thought of my husband at the vet's speaking soft words to the cat as he was put down was too sad. It sounds awful, not only having to see an animal you have loved fade away, but also having to give the command. When do you decide that it's time? How do you say the words? When Jenny Diski wrote about putting down her cat, she had to be told by the vet that it was OK to stop holding him, that the cat was dead.

Poor husband. Poor Scampie.

According to Murakami, 'Family – even if that includes cats too – is a living thing that has a certain balance, and when one corner of it falls apart, it doesn't take long before everything subtly breaks down.'

Men who love cats are generally quieter about it. Kerouac, Burroughs, Picasso, Matisse, Churchill, Murakami . . . the list of culturally significant men who have loved and lost cats without shame is long. That love certainly carries less cultural baggage. In *La Chatte*, Colette writes of a young marriage broken up by the wife's jealousy of her husband's love for their cat. It was something of a role reversal: in the real world, Colette was the cat lover. 'When I enter a room where you're alone with animals, I feel I'm being indiscreet,' her husband said.

My mother says that one of the few times she saw my dad cry when they were young was when the family cat died. Hemingway put his cat, Mr Willie, out of its misery in typical macho fashion – by holding a gun to its head –

but wrote in a letter afterwards: 'Have had to shoot people before but never anyone I knew and loved for eleven years. Nor anyone that purred with two broken legs.'

Kerouac, meanwhile, wrote: 'It was exactly and no lie exactly like the death of my little brother – I loved Tyke with all my heart, he was my baby who as a kitten just slept in the palm of my hand.'

When I got married, my grandmother gave me some advice. 'Men are far more vulnerable than you realise,' she said. She was not identifying a weakness so much as warning me how they might hide their sadnesses, how we shouldn't always assume that they are strong. I felt sad that it was my husband who was selected, or selected himself, to take Scampie to be put down. I knew that he had done it to save the women in the family from additional pain, that in his male way he had taken charge of the situation, and that this had been a kind thing to do. He is a very kind man, my husband. I also knew that, in many ways, Scampie felt like his cat, his partner in crime when he was exiled to the annexe, his escort after dark. I understood perfectly his reasons for wanting to do it, but I still wish he had been spared the ordeal. I have been with a cat as he crossed the threshold between life and death, and it is not something you forget, especially not when it's on your say-so.

It does not surprise me now that, looking back, I spent so much of my twenties worrying about death that I could not turn my thoughts to birth.

After leaving home, I thought I had been freed from the work of caring, but I ended up looking after someone else's children. Those children taught me a lot, both in terms of French grammar and child development, not to mention the importance of the social relationships we form outside our own families. Aurelie and her two eldest came to my wedding; two years before the pandemic, she invited me to their house in Provence, along with her two youngest, and I drank rosé and ate her mother's delicious cooking, and, in the fading sunlight, as the scent of lavender filled my nostrils, swam in the cold, cold water of a nineteenth-century swimming pool that the kids wouldn't go near because it hadn't warmed up yet.

Even after departing Paris and spending my twenties truly without caring responsibilities, the work didn't stop; it just changed shape. Instead of blaming myself for 'sleeping through' the motherhood question, I have come to understand that I was simply engaged in other labour: activism, writing and talking and campaigning about violence against women, as well as disability rights, poverty, and other forms of injustice.

You can express love through politics, and through work

in your community. It can be expressed as part of a collective, in the myriad social relationships that exist between people.

In *The Mother of All Questions*, Rebecca Solnit writes that:

> One of the reasons people lock into motherhood as a key to feminine identity is the belief that children are a way to fulfil your capacity for love. But there are so many things to love besides one's own offspring, so many things that need love, so much other work love has to do in the world.

In the year of lockdown, I have felt the desire to express that love more than ever. I know that, whether I have a child or not, I will never be short of it. Maybe it will happen for me, maybe it will not, because even if I choose it – and I think, I really think, I might choose it – it may not choose me. I know that I am capable of finding great meaning in a life without motherhood, and that I am capable of finding great meaning in a life that contains it.

And I know that the women who make the other choice are my sisters and not my enemies; that their lives will be as rich and as meaningful as mine.

~

What is your purpose?

Annie Ernaux writes: 'Maybe the true purpose of my life is for my body, my sensations and my thoughts to become writing, in other words, something intelligible and universal, causing my existence to merge into the lives and heads of other people.'

She is harking back, I think, to Hélène Cixous, who said that it is only by writing herself that a woman can 'return to the body which has been more than confiscated from her, which has been turned into the uncanny stranger on display'.

Trauma has kept my body a prisoner for too long, I realise. It has prevented me from pursuing so many of the things I long for: most of all, a child. We have been in a battle that has lasted for years, and I know I cannot be the only one.

I know that there is a risk involved in allowing my body and thoughts to become writing, but I must do it all the same. I will never live without fear, but if I give it a shape, maybe others like me will start to find the words for their experience.

When I think of becoming a mother, I am beginning to think of doing so without anxiety, and I can only really put this down to this year of the cat. It's ridiculous that a small, furry feline named after a fish should have had this effect, but it's true.

I am not cured. I dislike much of the narrative around

mental illness and facing your fears, though in the end it was exposure therapy that helped lessen my terror of the outside world. (Whether this will work for the cat is another question altogether. I suspect she's indoors for good and likes it that way.) In a way, caring for the cat has acted as a kind of exposure therapy.

'Survivors of trauma often begin to fear that they are damaged to the core and beyond redemption.' I remember reading this, in *The Body Keeps the Score*, and feeling recognition.

Taking care of Mackerel has taught me that I am not beyond redemption, nor am I irrevocably damaged. It has taught me that you can look after someone – or something – and that instead of consuming you, it has the potential to inspire.

A child has the potential to inspire me even more, just as caring for my brother has shaped me in so many ways. Hard though it has been, I consider his presence in my life to have been a gift. He has taught me so much. I am a kinder person because of him. I am, I think, a better writer because of him, too.

And, in turn, maybe I can inspire a child. Maybe, instead of looking on my past as something that has caused me illness and pain, and which will inevitably cause my child illness and pain, I can start to see it as a legacy that could help me be a better, more caring parent, and give her the happiest life I can.

A cat is not a baby. I know this. All the same, I have put so much love into this animal. I have held her in my arms and, when the longing has become too much, I have wept into her fur. She has allowed me to give voice to all the feelings that I could never have admitted to before: to fear and ambivalence and self-hatred, and above all, a caring impulse that I had banished from my being. For years, I was free and only had to look after myself. Not that I always did that.

I took risks, liberties, the occasional substance. I needed that time.

I am not 'cured' of my fear of motherhood, or of the mental illness that could resurface if I embark upon it, but I am hopeful. It is a hope that I have been lacking all this time, when I think about the world and the future terrors that it faces. I have realised that having a child can be an act of hope, too. For me, it is also a decision that requires no small amount of bravery, but with that need for courage, I now also feel excitement. Could I really be a mother? The thought makes me want to laugh and also dance.

Not long after he comes home, my husband and I return from lunch and decide to sit in the garden, drinking wine in the sun. (Mackerel is sleeping in a patch of kitchen window-light, untempted by the fine weather.) Last week, I had my first dose of vaccine – the stipulation to wait several months before trying for a baby has been removed thanks to more data – and I am feeling celebratory.

As we drink, we play music that makes us think of spring. Karen Dalton asks us if we're leaving for the country, because the city brings us down, and that question hovers over our rented lives as it has for years now, but it does not trouble us today. Who knows what our situation will look like in the future? Who cares? I am happy, and when it starts to rain, I am happier still.

I think of how it rained the day we brought the kitten home a year ago, and how we sheltered from the downpour, unaware of what those months would have in store for us, how they would shape us in ways that could play out for the rest of our lives. As we sat eating our sandwiches, we didn't think of the death or illness or mental anguish that seemed to be engulfing the world, only of the small creature mewing herself to sleep next to us. She needed us, and we needed her.

It is that late spring, early summer rain that falls in heavy droplets, but my husband and I do not go inside. We carry on sitting there and drinking, laughing at the weather, getting wetter and wetter. Together, grateful, in love. Upstairs, blissfully dry, the cat snoozes on and will until feeding time, when she'll run delighted into my lap, purring, as she always does.

Summer (coda)

Recovery rarely operates on a straight line. Just as I start to think that I am coming out of a bad patch, mental-health-wise, catastrophe strikes.

Mackerel and I are playing with her favourite bird toy when I notice that, in a flash, the string has broken and a not-insignificant portion of it has vanished.

'Fuck,' I say. 'Mackerel darling, did you eat it?' I knew this moment would come, eventually, and I know now how it will play out. My worst-case scenario has come to pass: curiosity will actually kill the cat. I try to open her jaw to see if it is wrapped around her tongue, but she scarpers.

A 'linear foreign body', as it is called when a cat swallows a piece of string, cotton, or elastic, is the thing every cat owner is taught to dread from the moment you bring them home. In a worst-case scenario, it can wrap itself around the cat's internal organs and kill them.

To say that I am panicking is an understatement. I work out how much string she has swallowed – at least a foot, maybe two – and phone the vet. 'You'll need to bring her in so we can try and make her sick,' they say.

It is 8pm on a Friday night. My husband is away, and Mackerel is now too big for her cat carrier. I had bought another one, but it is yet to be assembled. While Mackerel hides somewhere in the house, no doubt sensing the change of atmosphere that always coincides with a visit to the vet, I try and put the case together on the floor. It takes, inexplicably, an hour and a half. For some reason, the pieces just won't click together. I swear throughout, or at least until I start weeping.

Getting Mackerel into the carrier is the first challenge. She is lurking deep beneath the bed, far from reach. When I do manage to tempt her out and grab hold of her, the moment she sees the cat carrier, she wriggles free of me in a twisting motion that would be impressive were it not so maddening. Finally, at midnight, I get her in by wrapping her in a little towel and call a cab.

Mackerel cries throughout the entire journey, and I cry throughout the wait at the animal hospital. Sitting there in my nightgown, sobbing into my face mask, I have become the essence of crazy cat lady. It is a complete overreaction, but I can't seem to stop. It's as though the cat is the last thing standing between me and a total breakdown. It is only now that I realise the extent to which she has kept me sane.

The vet comes out and tells me that the emetic didn't make Mackerel sick, it simply sent her to sleep. *For Christ's sake, Mackerel*, I think. She will dry-heave dramatically at the mere sight of a worming tablet, but won't throw up when it's really needed.

'She's all curled up,' the vet says. 'She's very sweet.'

I am told that it is fifty-fifty on whether they need to operate. In the meantime, I am sent home to investigate all her turds for signs of string.

The next morning, having slept fitfully next to an extremely loving, purring cat (she is at her most affectionate after a brush with the veterinary establishment), I glove up and embark on this unenviable task. Lo and behold, there is string. Not very much, but some.

'Well done, Mackerel!' I say. But my joy is short-lived. For the next two days, she doesn't shit. I try putting her in her litter box, but she just looks at me. We are in a stand-off. I google cat laxatives and home remedies, and decide I can't face the fallout.

'I can't ever be a mother,' I say to my own mother, on the phone. 'I can't even cope with a sick cat.'

I have been having a constant anxiety attack for the past seventy-two hours. I am exhausted. Mackerel, meanwhile, seems fine, though somewhat baffled that there is suddenly so much focus on her toilet habits.

In the end, I phone the vet again. A nice woman answers, and I explain the situation. 'You had better bring her back in.'

They will need to scan her, and probably operate.

I start crying again. 'I'm sorry,' I say. 'I don't know what's wrong with me.'

'You're a mum,' the woman says. 'It's normal to worry about your baby.'

Oh, Christ, I think. *I am not a mum. I am so far from being a mum.* An image flashes into my mind of my brother on the ground, paramedics, my own mother. *That's being a mum,* I think.

Instead, I say: 'Thank you.'

The bill will be around £900, on top of the £400 I have already paid. I realise with surprise that I don't care. In that moment, I would pay anything for her to live.

I am wrestling her into the cat carrier when she performs the twisting move yet again. She sprints the entire length of the house and shoots into her little box like her arse is on fire and shits, finally, triumphantly, as though her freedom – emotional, spiritual, rectal – depends on it.

Afterwards, I will reflect that, hysterical though I may have been, I did everything that I could to keep that cat alive, and I will feel, though slightly embarrassed, a sense of real achievement. But for now, I focus on praising her.

'You're a good little cat,' I say. 'What a good little cat you are.'

The line on the test reads positive.

I stare at it, counting backwards, retracing our movements.

It just doesn't seem feasible. Although I had symptoms, I had assumed that they were down to the second dose of vaccine. I was only really testing on the off-chance.

My hand is shaking.

I walk out of the bathroom, to where my husband is waiting in the bedroom.

'It's positive,' I say, weakly.

In shock, that afternoon I look at paintings of the Annunciation, searching for ones that feature cats. It is the sort of picture research exercise that I enjoy, and it has a calming effect. I have always loved Annunciations, though I am not at all religious.

(I came to appreciate religious painting when I lived in Italy, in a residence that used be attached to a seminary. There was a painting of the Madonna and Child above each student's bed. Mine was by Botticelli: *The Madonna of the Book* (1481). Most of my friends took theirs down, but I left mine up. In it, Mary looks as if she's trying to read the book, but the Christ child on her knee keeps blocking her view.)

The Annunciation that I find today is from 1491, a fresco from a church in Brescia, Lombardy, painted by Giovanni Pietro da Cemmo, about whom little is known. His Mary bears the angel's news with solemn serenity, her face downcast, her hands clasped together in prayer. At her feet is an hourglass, a pair of amusingly modern-looking high-heeled mules, and a small black kitten.

Later, I take another sort of test, to be sure. I wait for five minutes, but I already know the result.

'Pregnant,' it says. Irrefutable.

I have been drawing the Empress from the tarot deck for weeks.

That evening, still in shock, I look again at the black kitten in the painting. Is it intended to represent demonic evil, as a counterpoint to the angel's presence? Is it the Virgin Mary's 'shadow self', the dark, arcane side of the mother-goddess? Or is it an ominous forewarning of catastrophe that will befall this expectant mother and the baby inside her?

The black cat seems so sweet and harmless; but then we are told that the devil comes in many guises.

There are so many ways of seeing. Brimming with the news of my own personal windfall, I decide to interpret the presence of the little cat another way: as a symbol of luck. An unexpected miracle. A friend.

Author's Note

I am indebted to the authors of the following works: Alice Maddicott's *Cat Women: An Exploration of Feline Friendships and Lingering Superstitions* (September Publishing) reminded me of Gwen John's fondness for her cat, which I first learned of as a young school pupil, and contains haunting photographs of women and their cats which sat in my mind's eye as I wrote. Marie-Louise von Franz's *The Cat: A Tale of Feminine Redemption (Studies in Jungian Psychology, 83)* (Inner City Books) was invaluable in terms of archetypes and goddesses. Thanks also to Nick Bradley, the author of *The Cat and the City*, for recommending it. *Revered and Reviled: A Complete History of the Domestic Cat* by L. A. Vocelle provided me with the early news reports of cat hoarding, and a broader timeline of the cat's role throughout history. *The Cat in Art* by Stefano Zutti (Abrams) and *The Cat in Photography* by Sally Eauclaire (Chronicle Books) helped to provide the visual background for my writing.

Mary Gaitskill's *Lost Cat* (Daunt Books) is a masterpiece of cat writing, and the lingering questions I was left with as a reader got me thinking about the different forms of love and care we all experience. Doris Lessing's *On Cats* (Harper Perennial) helped reassure me that the cat can be a topic of serious literature. Antonia White's *Minka and Curdy* showed me the playful side of cat writing, as did *La Chatte* by Colette. Alice Walker's 1997 essay 'Anything We Love Can Be Saved', extracted in *On Cats: An Anthology* (Notting Hill Editions), and Sam Leith's 'She was just a damn cat, but I loved her', *Spectator*, 18 July 2020, were also inspirational.

I am grateful to Silvia Federici, whose *Caliban and the Witch* made me see the witch hunts in a new light, and took this book in an unexpected but fruitful direction.

The writing of Elena Ferrante, particularly *Frantumaglia*, Annie Ernaux, Adrienne Rich, Rebecca Solnit, Sheila Heti, Heidi Julavits, particularly *The Folded Clock*, and Hélène Cixous all inspired my thinking about what it means to be a woman writing motherhood, and not-motherhood, and reassured me that, as ever, the personal is political.

Sylvia Plath's 'Ella Mason and Her Eleven Cats', Margaret Atwood's 'February', Fleur Adcock's 'The Inner Harbour', and Lydia Davis's 'A Double Negative' are all cited in the text.

Finally, thank you to all the friends, family and strangers who generously shared their stories of cat love with me, and allowed me to repeat them here.

Artworks referenced or alluded to

Bronze figure of Bastet with a litter of kittens, British
  Museum, 900BC–600BC.
The Whittington Stone, Archway, London, 1821.
'I Can Haz Cheezburger?', meme, 2007.
Breakfast at Tiffany's film poster, Robert McGinnis, 1961.
Champfleurette, the White Cat, Louise Bourgeois, 1993.
'HI, WE UNDERSTAND YOU ARE 40 AND STILL NOT
  MARRIED', meme, origin unknown.
Cat Women, Brooke Hummer, 2010.
The Bottesford Witches and their familiars, from *The
  Wonderful Discovery of the Witchcrafts*, 1691.
Girl with a Cat, Gwen John, 1918–22.
Young Woman Holding a Black Cat, Gwen John, c.1920–5.
Cat, Gwen John, 1904–8.
Raminou Sitting on a Cloth, Suzanne Valadon, 1920.
Jeune Fille au Chat, Suzanne Valadon, 1919.
Lois Mailou Jones painting in her studio, photographer
  unknown, c.1938.
Leonor Fini and Cat, Martine Franck, Paris, 1981.

La Grande Parade des Chats (The Great Parade of the Cats), Leonor Fini, 1973.

Self-Portrait, Gertrude Abercrombie, 1934.

Tracey Emin and Docket, Tracey Emin, 2005.

Lost Cat Poster, Tracey Emin, 2002.

How it Feels, Tracey Emin, 1996.

Joni Mitchell with her kitten, 2020, photographer unknown.

Femme/Maison, Louise Bourgeois, 1946–7.

Rooms Designed for a Woman, Emily Speed, 2017.

Barbara Hepworth with her cat Nicholas and her sculpture 'Reclining Form (Rosewall)' by Ida Kar, 1961.

Mên-an-Tol, Bronze Age.

Madonna del Parto, Piero della Francesca, after 1457.

Annunciation, Jan de Beer, 1520.

Annunciation, Lorenzo Lotto, 1534.

Annunciation, Barocci, 1592–6.

La Madonna del Gatto, Barocci, 1575.

Cartoon strip, Anna Härmälä, 2021.

WSPU poster, 1914.

The Madonna of the Book, Sandro Botticelli, 1480.

Annunciation, Giovanni Pietro da Cemmo, c.1491.

Acknowledgements

When I first started writing this book, I didn't quite know what it was going to become, or indeed that it would be a book at all. All I knew was that the words that were coming out felt true, and that the subjects that they touched on – art, caring, motherhood, trauma, fear and what it means to love – were things that I had been thinking about for much of my life. I am so grateful to Eleanor Birne for seeing the potential in this project from the start and for helping me bring it to fruition, as well as those at PEW Literary who have worked with her.

I cannot thank Mary-Anne Harrington, my editor, enough for her wisdom, guidance and insight. Working with a fellow cat woman was important to me, but I never dreamed that I would find one as brilliant as you – thank you, it has been an absolute dream. Everyone at Tinder Press has been wonderful – especially assistant editors Amy Perkins and Ellie Freedman. Thank you all, I feel very lucky to have Tinder as my publishing home. Special thanks to Anna Morrison for her beautiful cover design,

303

and illustrations. You have really brought Mackerel to life on the page.

I am indebted to early readers Holly, Sarah, and Jessica, who gave valuable feedback and the confidence to keep going. This book wouldn't have happened at all without Jacob, who listened to my idea for 'Crazy Cat Lady' – as it was then unofficially called – during a lockdown walk and didn't treat me like a madwoman. I know this isn't the book I thought I'd write, but I think it's better for it, and I hope you agree.

To my parents, I am grateful to you for your love, wisdom, and creative support, and for bringing so many cats into my life. Mum – I know you think I portrayed you far too positively, but you really are as magnificent as I wrote in the book, and I'm sure readers will forgive you for the occasional 'bloody cat!' Dad – I have loved the cat-related conversations that have flourished between us since Mackerel arrived on the scene. I am also grateful to my wider family, especially the 'Where's the Cat?' group chat members, and their feline companions.

But most of all, thanks are owed to my husband, Tim, for putting up with my persistent mortifying habit of writing about our lives: I hope that I have done that strange, sad, but at times wonderful year a kind of artistic justice. A week or so before I went into unexpected early labour, I found Basil the Hungarian Cat in the lining of an old handbag. He had, I thought, come back into my life at exactly the right time, and he was alongside me as a good luck charm throughout the, at times difficult, birth of our son. But that experience taught me that I didn't really need a good luck charm, because I had you.

To my blue-eyed boy: I wrote this before you existed, and when you come to read it one day you may have your own thoughts and feelings about it. Despite the fact that at times it may seem from my words that I had doubts about becoming a mother, I want you to know this: I loved you before I met you, and I always wanted you. Sometimes mums get scared, too, but I'm glad I did the brave thing. I haven't regretted it, or you, for the glimmer of a second.

Finally, to Mackerel, who changed my life, but cannot read: consider this an IOU for an extra special scratch behind the ears, and some fresh crab.